ARTAUD

FOR BEGINNERS®

GABRIELA STOPPELMAN

ILLUSTRATED BY JORGE HARDMEIER

Writers and Readers Publishing, Inc.
P.O. Box 461, Village Station, New York, NY 10014
sales@forbeginners.com

Writers and Readers Ltd.
PO Box 29522, London N1 8FB England
begin@writersandreaders.com

Spanish Edition:
Artaud para Principiantes,
published by ERA NASCIENTE SLR
Arce 287, Buenos Aires (1426) Argentina

A Writers and Readers Documentary Comic Book®
Copyright ©2000

ISBN 0-86316-291-6
1 2 3 4 5 6 7 8 9 0

Manufactured in the United States of America

Beginners Documentary Comic Books® are published by Writers and Readers Publishing, Inc. Its trademark, consisting of the words "For Beginners, Writers and Readers Documentary Comic Books®" and Writers and Readers logo, is registered in the U.S. Patent and Trademark Office and in other countries.

Contents

Who am I? Where do I come from? I am Antonin Artaud... You will never forget me.

I'll change the rules of poetry and theatre forever. I want to close the gap between art and life.

Artist of Total Rebellion

HE REBELLED AGAINST EVERY IDEA that tried to conceal the true causes of human suffering. His life was itself an expression of despair. His art was a dramatic attempt to root out the causes of his despair. His poetry did not seek to explain. His theatre did not claim to represent.

His work was a great exercise in 'lucidity'. The lucid person could see the possibility of another reality. And to be lucid you had to be 'cruel'. Cruelty did not mean only destruction, but also discipline and determination in the way one lived one's life and what one believed in, even if that meant risking life itself. Even if the price were madness or death. Antonin Artaud, the man for whom barriers existed only to be overcome. His work invites you not to study or reflect, but to defy. If you are open to the experience, you can share in his total rebellion.

CHAPTER 1
A Poet's First Steps

The Irreverent Son

ANTONIN ARTAUD WAS BORN on 4 September 1896 in Marseilles. His mother, Euphrasie Nalpas, was of Greek origin. His father, a rich ship-owner, was descended from an ancient seafaring family. Antonin was the Artauds' first son. Until his birth, life had run smoothly enough. His mother took responsibility for managing the home and his father, Antoine, was often absent and, when at home, detached and preoccupied with work. But it wasn't long before problems arose. From a very young age, Antonin suffered from severe neuralgia, stuttering and intense headaches. At the age of four, meningitis brought him to the brink of death. His mother had only recently lost another son and so she tried everything to get Antonin to take his medication. Thus began the battles between mother and son.

That sweet's poisoned.

You must eat it. It will make you better. Your brother's death has already brought us enough pain.

Don't take any notice, doctor, he suffers with his nerves.

You don't understand people. That's why you can't make them better. My sister's death was all your fault.

I've done all I can do.

Childhood is like death.

Antonin was eight years old when his sister Germaine died aged only seven months. This bitter blow further aggravated his delicate health. He distrusted everyone who was unable to understand his real suffering. Although very young, he had already witnessed a great deal of pain and death. He understood that illness attacked not only the body but also the soul. No medicine could heal his pain, anguish and doubts.

For him, any physical illness was just a symptom of a much more serious malady: the inability to understand the cause of his own despair.

The adolescent Artaud began to develop artistic talents. He wrote poetry and sketched enthusiastically. At the age of fourteen he set up a literary magazine in which he published his first writings under the pseudonym 'Louis de Attides'. From those early pieces, he decided that poetry was the only possible form of existence. Not the simple fact of writing poems; poetry had to be lived every day and at every moment. For him, it meant risking life itself.

When I recite a poem I don't do it for praise, but to feel the bodies of men and women...I mean bodies, the physical materialisation of a being in poetry.

I don't trust reality. You can find truth in the secrets of dreams.

I believe that the poet must be a visionary. He must try to see what's hidden from most men.

Many of my poems in **Les Fleurs du Mal** are called immoral. I have to suffer both legal and social persecution.

Reading Rimbaud, Nerval and Baudelaire introduced him to a new world. These writers seemed to have broken all the rules of traditional poetry. At last Artaud had found what he considered fundamental to literature. He discovered not just the simple description of feelings, but a force in poetry that was as intense as life itself. Impressed by these readings, Artaud was curious to find out more about the authors. He discovered that all three had had difficult lives and tragic deaths. Nerval, after much suffering, committed suicide. Rimbaud abandoned his poetry very young and set off for Africa, where he trafficked in arms and slaves and eventually died of cancer of the knee. Baudelaire struggled all his life against poverty and his addiction to alcohol and drugs.

Artaud's reading stimulated a passion for poetry. These writers not only introduced him to the company of good literature; Antonin considered them his accomplices—they shared his ideas and his suffering. He realised that the path of poetry could only be travelled if he were prepared to risk everything.

To write poetry is to write oneself. To read poetry is to read oneself.

At seventeen, Artaud was a young man full of questions with no answers. His home life got worse; arguments with his mother would end in terrible nervous crises. Each time a doctor arrived at the house to treat Artaud, a family conflict would be triggered, but his mother would not give in. Of her nine children, only three had survived infancy and she placed her faith in medicine to help her eldest child. His father, on the other hand, showed no interest at all. He thought that Antonin should follow him in his career as ship-owner and sailor. But Antonin did not do as his father wished. In 1913 he revealed his desire to be ordained as a priest though he eventually abandoned the idea.

To be a priest or to dedicate himself to literature? These were the options which Artaud saw as a way of finding answers to his questions. He wanted to investigate the root of pain and discover what the barriers were that separated body and soul. He struggled to rid himself of those barriers but the choices the world offered did not satisfy him. He had to invent his own rules and fight on his own. Already he had an inkling that the price of independence might be solitude.

INSTITUTION

The church is an institution with its own rules. I'm not good at following orders. I must be free to discover the meaning of the word 'sacred.'

I must invent a new voice for speaking and a new voice for writing. I need to separate myself from everything I've already done and begin again. I must also remake my body. A complete physiological transformation.

The young poet lived in a state of permanent tension. He moved from deep depression to intense rage, episodes which would end in convulsions. Artaud tried to continue writing and reading poetry, but his body gave him no peace. In 1915, a nervous breakdown caused him to burn many of his poems.

Artaud's parents decided to have him committed to a clinic near Marseilles. But the doctors still could not find a cure. Severe neuralgia forced him to spend several periods in clinics. He was given large quantities of drugs and different illnesses were diagnosed, but to no avail. Indeed, Artaud became more entrenched In his views: he alone would be capable of finding a solution to his suffering. In order to ease the physical pains, he had to purify his soul.

Artaud's body did not respond at all well to his attempts to purify his soul. After another relapse, he was sent to a clinic in Switzerland where he remained for nearly two years. When the doctors realised they could not alleviate Artaud's physical pain, they prescribed opium. The drug brought relief and from then on, Antonin resorted to opium each time he had a spiritual crisis. But opium did not cure the cause of his illness, it merely soothed the pain. The drug became a refuge, never a solution and he was well aware of that. He tried to struggle against the addiction—a struggle that would continue until his death.

In 1920, back in Paris, he was under the care of Dr Toulouse, a psychiatrist well known for his particular interest in the mechanism of genius and artistic creation. During that time, Artaud continued to write poetry. He also painted and sketched. The doctor was drawn to the quality and lucidity of his work and suggested that he publish some poems and articles. Artaud agreed. His work appeared in the periodical *Demain* founded by Dr Toulouse.

CHAPTER 2
Surrealism

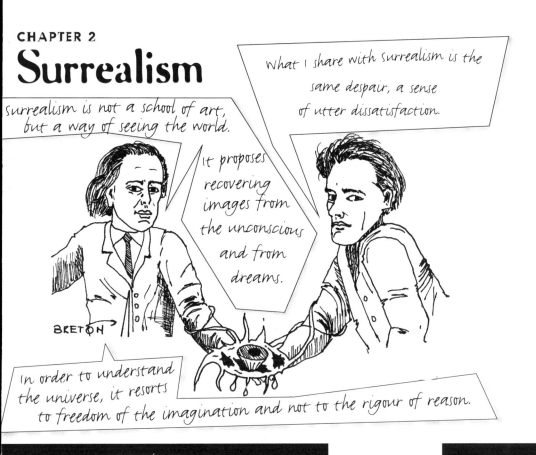

Surrealism is not a school of art, but a way of seeing the world.

What I share with surrealism is the same despair, a sense of utter dissatisfaction.

It proposes recovering images from the unconscious and from dreams.

BRETON

In order to understand the universe, it resorts to freedom of the imagination and not to the rigour of reason.

DURING THE AUTUMN OF 1920, the poet Max Jacob put Artaud in contact with important figures in the Surrealist movement. At first, he was enthused by the idea of finding himself amongst others who shared the same ideals. The sense of a common struggle brought a feeling of security. However, it did not take long for him to see that not all the Surrealists were fighting for the same cause. He knew that his own struggle was different from that of his companions. Nevertheless, this initial contact with the Surrealists had a significant influence on Artaud: all his work from then on bore the stamp of Surrealism.

The Surrealist movement represented a major attempt to liberate man. Artaud could not ignore this call to rebellion. The idea of rejecting all established values and of rebellion attracted him and he also supported the movement's ideology which was against the authoritarian figures of the father and the family. During those early years of Surrealism, Artaud was defining his own ideas on revolution. Revolution did not imply a change from one state to another. For him, true revolution meant the destruction of the old and rebuilding from nothing.

Artaud, a different kind of actor

1920 was a decisive year for Artaud, and not only because of his links with the Surrealists. It was also the year when he first performed on stage. Dr Toulouse remained sensitive to the artistic concerns of his patient and introduced him to the theatre director Aurélien-Marie Lugné-Poë who immediately recognised Artaud's extreme sensitivity. He also understood the problems which troubled him. He was fully aware of his need to take opium to ease the physical pain.

The start of Artaud's acting career was made difficult by his nervous shakes and his stuttering. But those obstacles were very quickly overcome and the first roles that he performed impressed Lugné-Poë. The following year, the director staged a play and did not hesitate to give Artaud a small part.

Who is this Artaud? What an odd bloke!

THEATRE

I don't know. I don't know him. But his acting is so strange. He looks as if he's praying or calling on some god or other.

The poses, the gestures, the make-up that Artaud uses aren't those of a beginner. For him performance is almost sacred. He seems the only true artist in a group of mere actors.

Artaud developed a performance style which depended more on gesture, atmosphere and space than on text and words.

I'll dedicate myself exclusively to the theatre as I conceive it. A theatre of blood. Theatre is, in reality, the genesis of creation.

Those early experiences were enough to awaken in Artaud an almost fanatical and religious enthusiasm for the theatre. His dedication was incredible and he paid minute attention to all the details of the production. He demanded of theatre the same that he asked of good poetry: 'to throw the whole body into it'. He believed that the more one demanded of one's body, the more freely the soul could reveal itself. All his work was aimed at stimulating a total reaction in the spectator. That is, not only an emotional response, but also a mental, spiritual and physical reaction. He wanted to offer the audience the possibility of 'experiencing' the birth of something new in the theatre. With each scene he wanted the observer and the actor to feel as if they were at the beginning of the world.

The theatre of Charles Dullin

Artaud met Charles Dullin, the director of the Atelier Theatre, through an actor friend. Dullin invited him to join his cast and Artaud accepted. He left his work with Lugné-Poë and completely dedicated himself to working with his new manager. Dullin had much in common with Artaud. Both had tried at one time to become priests. Both were critical of the contemporary conventional theatre. Both sympathised with Surrealist ideas. From the beginning, Dullin gave Artaud the opportunity to develop in every area he considered important for an actor. He not only allowed him to explore his acting ability but he also encouraged him to take responsibility for the design of costumes and sets. Artaud excelled himself in the creation of clothes and props. But not everything at the Atelier went smoothly...

It isn't easy to integrate Artaud into the company. He always tries to impose his own ideas. His performances don't fit in with my productions. This creates conflict with the others.

I'm not talking about philosophical reasoning, but a thinking process that goes from the inside out, from the empty to the full. I call the knowledge of this thought 'poetry'.

To think = poetry

ENDING
ENDING
ING·END
ENDING·EN
ENDING
ENDI·END
END·ENDI
EN·ENDIN
END·ENDIN
ENDING·END
ENDING·END
ENDING·END

Dullin suggested improvisation techniques for his students: the actors were not to represent their conflicts, but to 'think them through their souls'. 'Thinking' involved a different activity from logic or mere reasoning. To think was to give life. Artaud got more from these improvisations than from any other exercise. He gesticulated in an exaggerated way, he distorted his voice, he simulated convulsions through his whole body. He was fascinated by the new interpretation that Dullin gave to the concept 'to think'. Artaud carried this idea to the extreme. He criticised any

possibility of thought that used words. Words carried within them fixed meanings. And meaning could not be fixed. To liberate meaning, you had to free thought from words.

A thought formed by 'endings' is, as the word suggests, something final, something with a fixed meaning. The thinking that Artaud called 'poetry' had nothing to do with the actual structure of poems. He wanted to find a language suitable for the theatre. He believed that words belonged to literature and that theatre had to liberate itself from words to find its true language.

Oriental theatre

Dullin infected Artaud with his fascination for oriental theatre. A Japanese theatre group arrived in Marseilles in 1922. Influenced by his mentor, Artaud attended a performance. The Japanese performed in front of a reconstructed temple. Enormous, brightly-coloured masks with black hair were hung from the walls. Such scenery surprised Artaud. He was amazed by the way that the Japanese actors used the physical resources of the set. Nothing was left out: neither music, gesture, nor full use of the scenery. Oriental theatre wasted no theatrical possibility, whether physical or psychic. The West needed to learn this lesson. Western actors and directors abused texts and depended on words because they were unaware of the expressive power of other methods.

Fitting into Dullin's company became more difficult. The main problem was that Artaud refused to repeat scenes—making rehearsals virtually impossible. For him, each interpretation had to be unique. Each performance was an unrepeatable act of creation. Like the genesis of the world, each scene was born just once. The philosopher, Jacques Derrida was emphatic on this point:

DERRIDA

Artaud wanted to eliminate all repetition. Theatre representation is finite, and leaves behind it, behind its actual presence, no trace, no object to carry off. It is neither a book nor a work, but an energy, and in this sense it is the only art of life.

FUNCTION DOES NOT REPEAT
FUNCTION DOES NOT REPEAT
FUNCTION DOES NOT REPEAT
FUNCTION DOES NOT REPEAT

It means that the actor keeps nothing in reserve, neither for himself nor for the next time. Repetition has become unacceptable to me. I can't go on working with the Atelier.

Letters to Génica Athanasiou

Génica Athanasiou, a Romanian, arrived in Paris in 1919. She was a strikingly beautiful woman. She came to France because she wanted to become an actress and she became Dullin's pupil. She met Artaud, probably in the autumn of 1921. Génica was the first woman with whom the poet had a sexual relationship. They worked together at the Atelier, and after Artaud left, she stayed with the cast until the 1925-1926 season. The relationship continued uninterrupted until 1927. Artaud very much admired Génica's dramatic potential and, above all, he valued her poetic grace, natural sensitivity and unusual Romanian charm. From the beginning of the relationship a regular correspondence between them was established.

Dear Génica,

You have a delicious soul. You write like no French person. Because you express yourself TOTALLY, you use phrases that a great writer would wish to put his name to. Don't be afraid of using words that don't go together. That's often how more can be expressed. There are times when the universe seems to surround me with an electric force. I no longer know how to deal with the pain.

Nanaqui

Nanaqui is the nickname I gave to my nephew, Antonin. It's Greek. When he was a child, he spent several holidays with me in Smyrna. It was up to me to teach him the language of my ancestors.

I often use the name 'Nanaqui' to sign the letters I send to those I love most, especially to Génica.

The correspondence between the poet and Génica carried on regularly until the couple broke up, and then less frequently until 1940. These letters were true pieces of poetry, in the way that Artaud conceived of poetry: total expression. In her letters Génica repeatedly reproached Artaud about his use of opium. He struggled hard against the addiction and tried numerous treatments, but his physical and psychological suffering made him lapse time and time again. That was one of the reasons for the breakup of the relationship.

In 1923, there began a period of intense artistic activity. Artaud searched for an answer to his spiritual doubts from any source that might inspire him. He decided to publish his first collection of poems, *The Heavens at Backgammon*, but after a while, he rejected it. He felt that the book did not truly represent him. He continued to meet with the Surrealists and tried to apply the ideas of the movement to his new theatrical experiences. After leaving the Atelier, he joined the company run by Georges and Ludmilla Pitoëff. There he continued his search for a new direction in theatre.

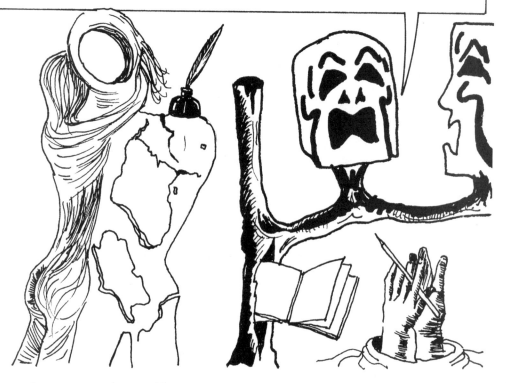

All Artaud's experience until now has brought him to one conclusion: art is life's double. Not daily life, but a life that is much more profound and true, which has yet to be discovered. A 'double' is not an imitation. Art is a reality, different, but as real as life itself.

Later on, Artaud would develop this idea more fully.

The Editor, Jacques Rivière

When he was twenty-seven, Artaud sent some of his poems to the journal *Nouvelle Revue Française*. Jacques Rivière, the editor, politely rejected the poems. Artaud then tried to explain why he felt passionate about his writing. He knew that the poems would not be published, but he nevertheless felt an irrepressible need to write them. Thus began an important correspondence between the editor and the author, which continued for two years.

These letters are considered some of the greatest literary works of the early years of surrealism.

I'm impressed by the contrast between your extraordinary capacity to analyse yourself and the lack of precision of your poems.
Jacques Rivière

Dear sir,
I'm in constant search of my intellectual self. So when I grasp a form, I hold on to it, no matter how imperfect it is...I prefer one imperfect poem which is full of beauty to a perfect poem without any inner excitement.
Antonin Artaud

Jacques Rivière took part in this exchange of letters with enthusiasm. He found some extremely original material amongst Artaud's explanations and arguments. The editor offered to publish these letters in his journal and the poet agreed. He too was aware of the value of the ideas expressed in this correspondence. His problems resolving the conflict between intellect and soul were clearly visible. What interested him most was not how to write the perfect poem, but to discover the causes of his suffering, the suffering that restricted his ability to think and create.

During those years, Artaud felt that poetry could help to free him from his former way of thinking. He wanted to find a poetic way of fulfilling himself, to make his first word also his last word. Even in the briefest note, poetry needed to vibrate because it was life itself. His intention never changed. He approached writing like a life sentence, but also as a great opportunity for rebellion.

The odd couple: Artaud and cinema

During the same period as the correspondence with Jacques Rivière, Artaud began his career as a film actor. His relationship with the cinema was ambivalent. On the one hand, he believed that the cinema could transform itself into a revolutionary language. On the other, he was critical of the way it was being developed. What is clear is that the majority of films being produced did not fulfil Ar-taud's demands. Nevertheless, he tried to put his ideas into practice. He accepted several film roles such as Marat and Savonarola in Abel Gance's *Napoleon* and *Lucrecia Borgia* respectively, and Massieu in Carl Dreyer's *The Passion of Joan of Arc*. He also wrote screenplays, including *The Seashell and the Clergyman*, one of the seminal films of Surrealist cinema.

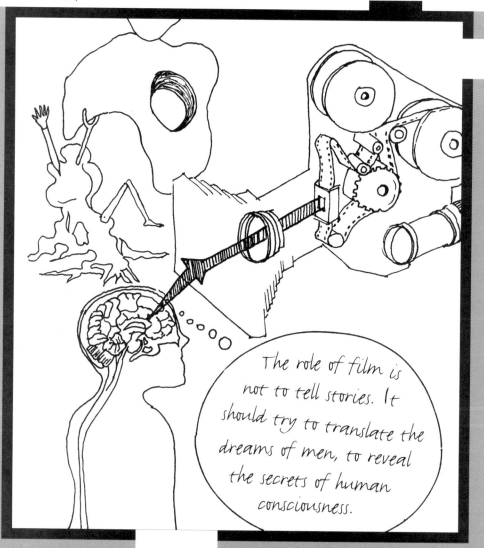

The role of film is not to tell stories. It should try to translate the dreams of men, to reveal the secrets of human consciousness.

Artaud proposes that cinema take the place of the human eye. But not an eye that simply reflects the world. He wants an eye that shows what's hidden from our everyday perspective.

Celluloid images have their own particular power that doesn't need to be reinforced by words. A good film must depend not on what's said, but on what's expressed. Expression means showing the invisible side of things.

Artaud's dreams were hindered by the advent of sound. He believed that words frustrated the spontaneous poetry of images. He totally rejected the technique of dubbing. However, cinema gave him the opportunity to earn a little money—but nothing more. What he considered to be authentic cinema had yet to be made.

Breton and Artaud—Accomplices

Around 1924, Artaud's relationship with the Surrealists became very intense. André Breton, the leader of the movement, invited Antonin to become more actively involved in the work of the Surrealists. Breton was fascinated by Artaud's ideas on theatre. They both agreed on the need to bring the extraordinary to the stage and to relegate literary texts to a marginal role. The Surrealists revived the ideas of Dadaism, an avant-garde movement which had preceded theirs. Its founder was Tristan Tzara.

I propose the destruction of bourgeois art. Theatre must go out onto the streets, even if it creates a scandal. For us, acting doesn't exist. We don't act. We **are**. The surrealists have taken this idea from us. They too are trying to mock bourgeois habits.

If you love Love, you'll love surrealism.
's rue   nelle, Paris

This is a visiting card typical of those traditionally sent by the bourgeoisie. Surrealists send them too, but they add jokes or ironic messages. They want to show the banality of many bourgeois practices.

For me, surrealism has never meant anything other than a new kind of magic...the intense liberation of the unconscious...The beyond, the invisible replace reality. The whole world no longer holds.

His views are too much, even for us. They are too confrontational.

Artaud has only been with us a short time but he throws himself into work with a kind of fury which infects the rest of the group. He is unforgiving. He lashes out again and again at the hypocrisy of society.

In this period the magazine La Révolution surréaliste was founded to spread the movement's ideas. Breton gave Artaud responsibility for editing the third edition, which appeared in 1925, and he gave it an unexpected spin. His writing was in the form of letters directed at the representatives of institutions against which the Surrealists were protesting.

In September 1924, Artaud's enthusiasm for the work with the Surrealists was overshadowed by the death of his father. It was a bitter blow. Until then, he had only shown feelings of rejection and hatred towards his father. Only on the day that he saw him die, did he feel able to reconcile himself with his father.

This death has made me see clearly that I must denounce all the lies that create suffering in men's bodies. All my art is but this protest.

Open letter to the world's rulers. My duty as poet is not to shut myself away to write. It is to go out and denounce your oppression which destroys men's bodies.
A.A.

Mature poetry

In 1925, Artaud published two books of poems: The Nerve-Scales and The Umbilicus of Limbo. The maturity of expression in these works was astonishing. Although his writing became no clearer, it seemed more alive. Artaud continued to emphasise his familiar themes: the need to liberate all that remained imprisoned by words and the impossibility of experiencing human language as a living force. But, above all, there was one constant mantra that was repeated in those writings: effectiveness.

The effectiveness of poetry is like a physical blow. This force comes from the greatest moral and physical suffering.

Artaud refuses to defend an ineffective culture that does not free man from hunger. Instead, he proposes to draw from culture ideas with a force as intense as hunger.

CHAPTER 3

Cruelty

The Alfred Jarry Theatre

By the time he was thirty, Artaud already had a vast experience of the theatre. And now differences began to arise with the Surrealists. Breton was highly distrustful of any theatre that depended on money to be produced. He believed that the pressure to attract funding restricted the freedom of the artist. But Artaud felt impelled to create something new. He desperately needed to find a place where he could put his ideas on theatre into practice. He decided, with Raymond Aron and Roger Vitrac, to set up the Alfred Jarry Theatre. The name was chosen as a homage to the brilliant and irreverent nineteenth-century French philosopher and dramatist. Jarry was seen by Artaud as the precursor to his own ideas on theatre. His character 'Ubu' was inspired by a grotesque schoolteacher ridiculed by all his pupils.

The first performance of my play Ubu Roi marks the beginning of the entire revolution in contemporary theatre.

ALFRED JARRY

UBU:
I AM THE THEATRICAL SYMBOL OF BOURGEOIS ABSURDITY.

PROGRAMME OF THE FIRST PERFORMANCE OF UBU ROI

The first *Manifesto* of the Alfred Jarry Theatre was published in 1926. The immediate effect was to aggravate the conflict with the Surrealists. Vitrac and Aron had already been expelled from the movement and the relationship between Artaud and Breton was coming to an end. Breton did not agree with Artaud's new projects and, for his part, Artaud rejected the Surrealist call to embrace Communism.

Our performances aren't directed at either the spectator's mind or his senses. They are aimed at his whole existence.

We want to be a part of the downfall of theatre as it exists now. The spectator cannot remain passive. He must be shaken, provoked, thrown into doubt.

Theatre isn't a game or a training school. The laws of dreams are projected onto the stage. That's the only trace of Surrealism in our project.

VITRAC

ARTAUD

ARON

The spectator who comes to our performances knows that... not only his mind but his senses and his flesh are at stake... and that he will not emerge unscathed. He must believe that we can make him scream.

It took more than six months to organize the theatre's first performance. The main difficulty was raising enough money and they solved the problem by selling the tickets in advance at the highest possible price. Finally the Alfred Jarry Theatre opened its doors.

The first performance, Burnt Belly, or the Mad Mother is a musical improvisation written by Artaud, with music by Max Jacob.

This improvisation is trying to express, with humour, the conflict between theatre and cinema.

While working on his projects for the new theatre, Artaud also had to deal with his personal problems. The physical pain continued and he could not stop resorting to opium. Génica Athanasiou urged him to try new detoxification treatments. Artaud agreed, but his attempts failed. Gén- ica decided to end their relationship and that decision sent Artaud into despair. He felt more alone than ever, abandoned by the only person who seemed to understand him. He found a little consolation in the possibility of work.

After our separation, I became for Artaud the figure who merges life and death. He both loves and despises me. That's what his occasional letters show.

I can no longer count on you in my torment since you refuse to accept the most affected part of me, my soul.
A. Artaud

Controversy with the surrealists

Artaud was finally expelled from the Surrealist group on 10 December 1926. Breton and his companions, Eluard, Aragon, Péret, and Unik published a pamphlet entitled 'In the Open'. This piece was littered with insults directed at Artaud. For the Surrealists of that era, revolution had to take place not only politically, but at every level. Breton insisted on the need to search for common objectives with the Communist Party struggle. Artaud refused to join the Party. Neither did he accept their methods. He held on to his idea of revolutionising the internal workings of the human soul as the first step necessary for any true revolution. The Surrealists considered this attitude to be cowardice.

In the Open

The surrealist movement has expelled that riffraff called Artaud. We are disgusted by all his activities. Not only his lack of political commitment, but also his literature and theatre. Artaud is an enemy of art. Only his personal interests are important to him. He is never prepared to risk anything essential for life or soul.

The surrealists

Artaud's view is that Marxism and Surrealism are irreconcilable. He agrees with our opposition to capitalism. He does not believe that Marxist ideology helps to lessen man's real suffering.

MARX

Marxists and Surrealists are revolutionaries who revolutionise nothing. They don't dare to attack the true causes of pain.

Artaud was not slow to respond. He did it through a manifesto, *In the Dark or the Surrealist Bluff*. Artaud did not personally attack any of the Surrealists. On the contrary, he made it clear that he continued to value much of the writing of his former companions. But he would not forgive them for trying to give revolution a merely practical significance. He accused them of clouding over the original true aim of the Surrealist adventure. Surrealism did not die for him the day that Breton and his followers decided that they had to affiliate themselves to the Communist Party; he decided he would continue the adventure alone. For Artaud, being a Surrealist was still a way to discover the secrets of man. Art could not become the propaganda instrument of a party. That would be its death.

The Alfred Jarry Theatre offers us, the audience, a complete spectacle. Cinema, music, dance and novel stage sets.

It's a pity that these shows have finished. There's nowhere else to go to see such original performances.

During the four years following his break with the Surrealists, Artaud continued to work with the Alfred Jarry Theatre, but between 1927 and 1930 he put on only four plays and a total of eight performances. Such scant production was not due to public hostility, but to the lack of financial resources. And Breton and his friends lost no opportunity to sabotage Artaud's work. They interrupted performances of the Alfred Jarry Theatre's third production in a scandalous manner. There were many obstacles and Artaud's theatre, one of the most revolutionary of the first half of the century, was on the point of closing its doors for ever.

Public hostility

The Alfred Jarry Theatre and the Public Hostility appeared in 1930 and was the theatre's last manifesto. Vitrac was responsible for most of the writing. Many of the passages were criticised for making too many concessions to the bourgeois public and that criticism was not entirely unfounded, but the truth was that Artaud and his friends needed financial help and that support would not come from the Surrealists. So the manifesto targeted a public of relatively rich intellectuals in the hope of obtaining their economic support. The piece was written with a particularly humorous and ironic tone which was typical of Vitrac. However, the Alfred Jarry Theatre had already given its final performance in January 1929. The manifesto came later and had no influence on Artaud's actual theatrical method. But it did create a basis for his future experiments in theatre.

Artaud has begun to share with us his thoughts on a project for a new theatre space.

ALFRED JARRY THEATRE

CLOSED

That's the end of this experiment but I'm going to take the best parts from it. For example, my idea of getting rid of the stage. The separation between the public and the performers is quite out of date.

The shock of Balinese theatre

Artaud continued his search for a new kind of theatre. He adapted different works by famous authors and published writings in which he tried to formulate new ideas. He dedicated himself to seeking out experiences that would help him clarify his thoughts. One of these defining experiences occurred in 1931 when Artaud attended a performance by a Balinese dance company. His old passion for oriental theatre was revived, and from that moment, all his confused ideas began to be consolidated in a new theory: The Theatre of Cruelty.

I want a theatre that offers total spectacle. Like the Balinese. Drama isn't developed between feelings, but between spiritual states. You can see the soul in the actors' bodies, in movement and staging.

Our theatre uses a new physical language, based on signs not words. Our movements are controlled and directed to be as effective as possible.

'Cruelty' has nothing to do with tearing each others' bodies apart but...

...it's to do with a much more terrible cruelty. The cruelty objects can practice on us. It reminds us that we are not free...

..and the sky can fall on our heads at any moment.

For Artaud, everything that acts is a form of cruelty. To act is to take the action to the limit. And in that case,

Cruelty = Life

The Theatre of Cruelty had to match life. But not each person's individual life, which was only the superficial appearance of his life. The function of the Theatre of Cruelty was to bring onto stage a reality different from the everyday, the reality of the extraordinary. The extraordinary was uncontaminated by ideas of morality and culture. It implied a return to a primitive consciousness, associated with ritual and the notion of magic. Magic could not be understood as simply tricks; magic allowed one to eliminate the false boundaries between body and soul. A theatre relying on this ritual language would use physical universal signs or hieroglyphics. It would act through enchantment. It would create its own reality. For that reason it was counter-productive to try to reproduce daily life on the stage. The core of the theatre proposed by Artaud was a complete rejection of imitation.

Art is not the imitation of life, but life is the imitation of a transcendental principle...

...which art puts us into communication with once again.

Imitation is an act of acceptance of the world as it is. The artist who imitates becomes an accomplice of that same reality that controls him. It doesn't allow man to free himself from his physical and spiritual ties. Art that has no sense of liberation, has no meaning.

A theatre of alchemy

Alchemy uses symbols and processes to transmute base metals into gold. But its true aim is not only to affect the tangible world, but also to transform the alchemist's soul.

Artaud proposes that the actor of the Theatre of Cruelty undergo a transformation similar to alchemy. An alchemy of the mind. The spirit transforms itself into gesture, movement, or into a cry.

A theatre of this kind would be forced to create its own language. Literature, music and all the other arts could contribute elements, but the bringing together of all these collaborative activities had to result in something entirely new. This was the work proposed by Artaud. The basic principles of this project were put forward in the *Manifestos of the Theatre of Cruelty*.

First Manifesto of the Theatre of Cruelty:
A new language, a new theatre

The first issue raised in the Theatre of Cruelty's *Manifesto* was that of language. Artaud's view was that the theatre would not recover its potential until it had found its own specific language. That implied that the effectiveness of the production should no longer depend on the written text. To transform theatre into the 'total spectacle' that Artaud proposed, it would be necessary to end the disproportionate respect given to literature and to dramatists' stage directions. Beneath the poetry of written works there was pure poetry, without form or text. The potential of poetry combined with effective theatre was greater than that of written poetry because theatre could call upon gesture, posture, expression, inflexion etc., resources specific to theatre. Even when gestures were repeated on the stage, they were never done in the same way twice. And so a fresh impact was guaranteed in each performance.

THEATRICAL LANGUAGE

Theatre must find a unique language halfway between gesture and thought...This language can be defined in terms of the possibilities of dynamic expression in space as opposed to the expressive possibilities of dialogue.

> House, aahh, grr, house, aahh, grr, house...

> The meaning of a word can almost be the opposite of its conventional meaning. The word 'house' is no longer just an obvious synonym for home or refuge. It can also indicate loneliness or desertion.

> spoken in this scene, 'house' loses its usual meaning. We have to discover its new significance in the context of all the actor's movements.

In the Theatre of Cruelty, the 'language in space' had to predominate over spoken words. Sounds and music entered, along with the visual support of objects, movements, postures. Words were simply transformed into signs, devoid of the meanings commonly given to them. They too became objects. They became part of a new theatrical language that the audience had to decipher, as with hieroglyphics.

Sacred theatre

For Artaud, the image of a crime projected
in a suitably theatrical setting had a more terrible
impact on the soul than merely portraying
the actual execution of that crime. He was convinced that the public thought above all with
its emotions, and so it seemed absurd to start off
by aiming to explain. Artaud was against the old
style of theatre that presented only psychological
conflicts. In the language of cruelty that he
proposed, an energy would be revealed that was of
a greater intensity than the force of life itself.

In search of a suitable technique

In the first *Manifesto*, Artaud did not give too many descriptions of techniques to be used in the theatre. He explained the objectives to be reached rather than the methods. The principal objective was to turn theatre into a function in the literal sense of the word: something that functioned like a perfect mechanism able to generate illusion and enchantment in the audience; a spectacle that allowed the audience to re-examine its internal and external reality. Every technique served the new theatrical language. The aim was to overcome the limitations of the word and produce a total creation on stage. There, man had to recover his real place in the universe—somewhere between dreams and events.

As actors we must stamp a precise physical rhythm onto our movements as if we were responding to a conductor and our bodies were a musical score.

Actors aren't slaves to the words of an absent author or an all-powerful director. Whether we act or organise the acting, we are all creators.

In the Theatre of Cruelty the production was in the hands of a single creator who had responsibility for both the play and the action. In this way the gap between author and director was eliminated.

Light, sound and costume

Artaud wanted the true effects of sound and lighting on the soul to be studied. The colour spectrum, hues, and effects that would allow lighting to be introduced, as if it were another character, had to be thoroughly reviewed. There would be one light for cold, one for anger, another for fear. As for music, ancient and forgotten instruments would be revived. The tonality of different metals and alloys needed to be investigated too, with the aim of producing unbearable or piercing sounds. Regarding costumes, Artaud was inclined to reject modern clothing in favour of the garments used for ancient rituals as they revealed a certain beauty linked to the primitive traditions that Artaud so much admired.

Every element on stage plays a central role. They're not merely decorations or adornments. Their choice cannot be left to chance. Everything must be significant.

The end of the stage

The distance between the stage and the auditorium needed to be eliminated in order to re-establish direct contact between the audience and the performance, the actor and the audience. The idea of the stage as a separate space where the play was performed went against the objectives of what Artaud saw as true theatre. This was one of the most revolutionary changes proposed. Artaud wanted to reformulate the whole idea of theatrical space. Space was not just related to an idea of place. Actors, masks, music, lighting movements, the situation of the spectator in relation to what he was watching, all this together formed theatrical space.

The spectator is placed at the very centre of the action. The performance moves around and through him.

No more scenery

Artaud insisted on banishing any idea of adornment on the theatrical stage. In its place he wanted to incorporate 'hieroglyphic characters'. This is what he called his effigies which were more than thirty foot high, musical instruments as tall as men and objects of unknown form and purpose that he incorporated onto the stage.

To subordinate the written word

The most important element, when choosing works for the Theatre of Cruelty, was to maintain the resolve not to interpret existing written plays. Artaud used themes, events and storylines from well-known works as a basis. But he transformed them according to his own taste and the demands of each performance. The very arrangement of the room, actors and audience, obliged him to make modifications to take full advantage of the space. The actor, when interpreting these plays, became one more element alongside all the other components of the scene. The success of the show still depended on the actor's skill, but he was not allowed any personal initiative. An actor could create total disaster in a production by improvising.

If I ask an actress to make a gesture of astonishment and her face shows terror, that inappropriate reaction can ruin the whole scene. The situation that she's interpreting may frighten her personally, but she should show only astonishment.

The first Theatre of Cruelty Manifesto closed with the description of an intended programme: the staging of well-known stories, such as The Fall of Jerusalem from the Bible, the story of Bluebeard and other myths and tales. Artaud repeated that he had no intention of following the written word faithfully. He even planned to get rid of the text altogether in some works, only keeping the costumes of the time, the settings and some characters. But, in the end, Artaud was unable to execute this program.

It has not been proven that a language superior to verbal language does not exist. Alongside the culture of words there's the culture of gestures.

The actor's gestures must be so intense that the spectator feels as if his skin has been pierced by an enormously powerful force. A force that transforms the spectator and the actor forever.

Cruelty is lucidity

The first *Manifesto* was published in October 1932. It appeared in the *Nouvelle Revue Française*, the same magazine that years earlier had published the correspondence between Artaud and Jacques Rivière. By 1932, Rivière was no longer the editor. Now the magazine was the responsibility of figures such as the poet Paul Valéry, the writer André Gide and Jean Paulhan. In a letter to Paulhan, Artaud refined the concept of cruelty even further.

> We must kill the father of ineffectiveness in theatre: the power of the word and the text. The text is the all-powerful god who will not permit true theatre to be born.

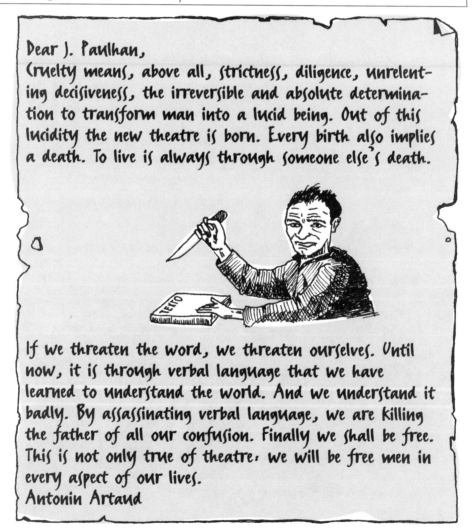

Dear J. Paulhan,
Cruelty means, above all, strictness, diligence, unrelenting decisiveness, the irreversible and absolute determination to transform man into a lucid being. Out of this lucidity the new theatre is born. Every birth also implies a death. To live is always through someone else's death.

If we threaten the word, we threaten ourselves. Until now, it is through verbal language that we have learned to understand the world. And we understand it badly. By assassinating verbal language, we are killing the father of all our confusion. Finally we shall be free. This is not only true of theatre: we will be free men in every aspect of our lives.
Antonin Artaud

At the end of 1932, the cumulative effects of drug dependency resulted in another nervous breakdown. Artaud was committed to a clinic in Paris for detoxification. The effect of this treatment was positive but short-lived. He would later suffer further periods of nervous crisis, but this temporary cure allowed Artaud to recover his strength and to complete the details of a Theatre of Cruelty production, The Conquest of Mexico. Being active and busy with the design of this show allowed Artaud to continue to explore the requirements of his new theatre more deeply.

In society every possibility of communication that man has open to him is a prison. I say a word to you to get something beneficial from you...

...and I reply with another word that will give me an advantage.

The Theatre of Cruelty does not share this theory of exchange. The production happens once and forever. It is not a re-presentation because it will not present anything again. The performance is not repeated because it is a unique energy that consumes itself in its present moment. The language used is a surrender, a gift that demands no reward.

Second Manifesto of cruelty

The *Second Manifesto* was published in 1933. In it more themes and techniques of the Theatre of Cruelty were defined. Greater clarity and maturity appeared in Artaud's ideas. In relation to the themes, he stated that his theatre would choose issues that corresponded to the agitation and unrest of the times, but it would do so in its own way by opposing the economic, utilitarian and technological state of the world. He aimed to bring back into style man's fundamental emotions throughout history. He preferred cosmic and universal themes taken from the most ancient mythologies: Jewish, Iranian, Hindu, and Mexican, amongst others.

Images of the monstrous throw into relief the fundamental conflicts of man.

The struggles between gods and men, chance and fate, natural disasters. All these obstacles profoundly affect man in his totality. From the start they separate out the false dilemmas of civilized man.

As for technique, the *Second Manifesto* placed great emphasis on the use of space. All levels of space would be used and all aspects of perspective, depth and height. This use of space would give the spectator a special notion of time. In a given time, the greatest number of possible moves would take place, combined with the greatest possible amount of physical imagery formed by a combination of objects, shouts, silences and rhythms that would create a true physical language.

The elements of this spectacle recapture the ancient meanings of popular festivals. There, the masks allow men to assume roles which are forbidden them by society.

The Theatre and the Plague

A couple of months after the publication of the *Second Manifesto of Cruelty*, Artaud gave a lecture at the Sorbonne called *The Theatre and the Plague*. But Artaud did not limit his role to that of a simple orator. He threw himself to the floor, shouting and sobbing as if he were a real plague victim. Many members of the audience laughed, mocked him or walked out. Artaud tried to draw a comparison between the effects of the plague establishing itself in a city and the effects of his Theatre of Cruelty.

When the plague has become established in a city, all normal social order collapses. The streets are choked with the dead. Vermin prowl amongst corpses. Plague victims wander through the city delirious and screaming. The smells and sights of the city become nauseating.

The disorder created by the plague awoke violent social forces that manifested themselves in an extreme form. Men crossed the boundaries established by morality and custom. In the delirium and desperation as they faced collective death, the darkest forces of the human mind were awoken. The gestures of men became extreme. The same would happen in the Theatre of Cruelty. The Theatre would recreate the conflicts that lie asleep within us with all their energy. That energy would appear on stage in the form of symbols. The function of theatre would be transformed into a battle of symbols. Both theatre and the plague obliged men to see themselves as they were. They uncovered the lie, they shook man out of his inertia.

The Theatre of Cruelty affects the audience's sensibility with all the horror of an epidemic.

> The images of plague show a spiritual energy at the point of exhaustion. Death has the final word in real life.

> Theatrical images tempt like a leap into emptiness. Spiritual energies are not exhausted because external reality isn't essential to theatre and it creates its own reality. The actor doesn't die. He submerges himself in the mysteries of death, as they appear in the depths of the human mind.

Artaud established one more comparison between the plague victim and the actor. Often, the plague would attack the human body externally, but the organs and entrails remained intact. The infected man would die with his internal organs undamaged although he would show all the outward signs of being destroyed. The same happened to the actor: his whole physical appearance might indicate that his life had been attacked by a violent evil, but his organism had not been affected. The true transformation was not visible to the human eye. The souls of both the infected man and the actor were changed for ever. In the first, the end was determined by physical death; in the actor a false reality was annihilated. This death allowed the discovery of a more authentic internal world

Heliogabalus

In 1934 Artaud wrote a biography of Heliogabalus, descendent of an Assyrian dynasty of sun-worshipping priests, the Basanidas. Heliogabalus was the name chosen by the main character when he was elected emperor of Rome at the age of fourteen. The name came from a god who belonged to an ancient cosmogony. The choice of a new name was a symbol of the emperor's intention. He wanted to change the ruling order in Rome and restore the spirit of the primitive people. The reign of Heliogabalus was very short. He was assassinated by his own guard.

did careful research to write this tale. For me, the life of this young emperor is an example of cruelty.

Artaud described the development of the cult of the sun god in the temple of Ernesa like a theatrical production. Its elements were placed according to the principles of cruelty. The shouts and the symbolic images and gestures gave life to a performance in which words had been left to one side.

I'm the god who appears in response to the invocation of the priests of the sun. My appearance is preceded by groans, shouts, the sounding of the gong and great disturbance amongst the people.

The rites of the sun were strangely mixed with the cult of the moon. The ritual showed the two principals, feminine and masculine. The intention of this ceremony was to recover the old unity of the whole. If the principals of the universe were separated, it was culture's responsibility. Rome belonged to a western culture that Artaud considered guilty of breaking up different unities: that of the unreal and the real, feminine and masculine, man and nature, art and life. For Artaud, Heliogabalus was the example of total revolution which he sought for all men. He rebelled against the gods and against the political power of Rome.

The rituals of sun-worship were charged with images of violent eroticism, brutal sacrifice and death. But this aggression was not gratuitous. It was a symbol of the spirit's war against itself. Men became warriors to end the division between the universal principles that governed the human spirit. These principles were forces. Divided forces caused man's alienation. To spill blood implied an act of purification.

Purification means the union of the real and the unreal, death and a means to life.

A fragmented culture multiplies its gods. They are all equal and must be worshipped as equals.

In unity there are no gods nor any necessity to name them. Universal principles are lived in a natural way.

For Artaud there was no difference between the idea of a god and the idea of a force. Europeans had created this distinction by giving the gods names. Anything that was named was dead because it was separated from the whole. Unity contained the contradictions between man and the universe. Every culture that tried to avoid its contradictions became fragmented.

Androgyny implies the fusion of the two sexes in one sole being. It's an image that appears in all ancient cultures.

Heliogabalus was the symbol of all human contradictions. He was at once the human king and the sun king. His religion was that of the masculine sun, but it was also that of the female moon. He himself wanted to be both man and woman simultaneously. Artaud described a ritual in which he simulated the castration of a man who appeared dressed as a woman. This represented the need to fuse opposites. Heliogabalus was not an idolator, but a magician. He held the powers of the rituals amongst which he had been raised.

The full title of Artaud's book was *Heliogabalus, the Crowned Anarchist*. For Artaud, to be invested with a sense of anarchy was to understand the effort needed to achieve unity. The division preceding the union of opposites implied great disorder. Heliogabalus, as king, found himself in the privileged position of being able to unify human difference. He achieved this using blood, cruelty and war. To be an anarchist was not to be a lover of disorder, but rather, to be a public enemy of the established order. And the Crowned Anarchist resented his own kingdom. He did not want to be a king in order to dominate; his desire was to use his power to transform the false harmony of things.

An anarchist is someone who holds out against every attack from the established order.

Heliogabalus destroys himself in order to transform himself into someone else. That is his strength, even when the power that he tries to destroy ends up assassinating him.

This power ultimately devours everything, even its defenders.

The coming of anarchy implied the arrival of poetry. In all poetry there was an essential contradiction. Poetry had to create great disorder, to bring about a clash of opposites. Out of that clash was born a new order. Turning poetry over to the world meant producing a state of applied cruelty, as understood by Artaud: the cruelty that objects acquired before being drowned. From the depths, these same objects were capable of unifying fire, gesture, blood and screams. The risk was great: whoever awakened this dangerous anarchy could become its first victim.

Heliogabalus was assassinated. His own guards destroyed him. First, they forced him to swallow his own excrement and then they hacked him to pieces. But death did not invalidate Heliogabalus' great achievement. He was the person responsible for bringing theatre and poetry to the Roman throne. He introduced change in the Emperor's palace. He expelled men from the Senate and put women in their place. For the Romans that was anarchy. For Heliogabalus it represented the re-establishment of the true law.

Disorder
Unity
Poetry
Rhythm
Greatness
Generosity

Order
Anarchy
Dissonance
Discord
Childishness
Cruelty

Just as life is theatre's double, Heliogabalus also does everything on two levels. Each of his movements has two faces.

At the end of the same year as *Heliogabalus* appeared, Gallimard, the prestigious French publishing house agreed to publish *The Theatre and its Double*. In order to comprehend Artaud's work, this is one of the most important books. In it, he refined the idea of the 'double'. The first mention of this theme had appeared in the Manifestos of the Alfred Jarry Theatre, but it was in *The Theatre and its Double* that his concepts were definitively explained. He specified that the theatre was the double of a reality which was not human. In that reality lay the universal principles which were born at the beginning of the world.

The universal principles can barely be glimpsed by the human eye.

Man had serious difficulties in approaching a reality so different from that of his daily life. This approach was also very dangerous. The danger lay in entering an unknown world where man could not use his usual excuses to avoid facing the truth. Even where the risk was great, it was worth searching for that experience. For Artaud, that was the only worthwhile objective.

The Theatre and its Double showed the development of Artaud's ideas. Collecting several articles in one volume brought different focuses on one central theme: the need to destroy the existing language in order to build another which would have a 'sacred' character. 'Sacred' meant reserved for, belonging and appropriate to the theatre. This task would not be easy. Not everyone would be able to make use of this language. Both the body and the spirit would need to be prepared.

The Theatre and the Plague

Production and Metaphysics

On the Balinese theatre

The Manifestos of Cruelty

The Theatre of Alchemy

This book brings together some of my articles.

From the beginning, the tone of the
book was violent and concise. The preface was called
'Theatre and Culture' and in it he again insisted on the
need to build a culture that connected with life.

The Theatre and its Double had to be understood as a book of protest. It protested against man's excessive worship of 'empty' forms. Artaud believed that if there was something evil and hellish in his time it was the cult of representation and signs as a way of knowing the universe. Culture was not a collection of articles to look at and enjoy from time to time. Culture was in action.

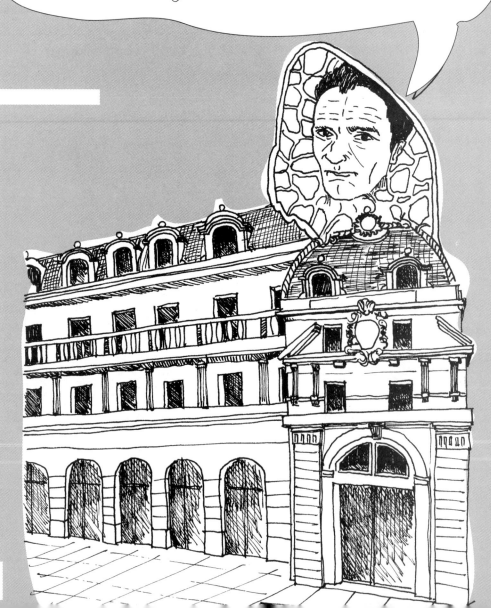

Culture isn't a pantheon or museum. It must be like a new lung for mankind. A second breath.

The Cenci

In May 1935, Artaud directed and acted in a performance of *The Cenci* adapted from a tragedy by the poet Shelley and a document translated by Stendhal. It was the story of the assassination of a sixteenth-century count by his own daughter. The topic of incest was of paramount importance to Artaud. He considered that the prohibition on carnal love between fathers and their children was the universal standard that assured the dominance of culture over nature. Moral standards were established by men with the aim of repressing the natural forces that tended to violate those standards. In that way, culture exercised control over human minds.

Scene from
The Cenci

The figures at the banquet are presented as animals to symbolise the bestial nature of society beneath its fine clothing.

Count Cenci's only ambition was to personify absolute evil. He held a banquet for the governors of the Church and State, in which he symbolically drank the blood of his children, thus mocking the ceremony of mass. God had destroyed his children, but the Count was God's accomplice since he had prayed for the death of his offspring. Cenci also raped his daughter, Beatrice, who was driven to plot against her father. Beatrice was imprisoned, tortured and then executed.

In *The Cenci* the movements performed by the actors on stage were perfectly geometrical. The characters moved around forming circles, parallels or triangles. These physical movements had very precise meanings. For example, the use of circles represented for Artaud the 'circular and closed world' of cruelty. It was a perfect form that did not permit any of the mistakes of conventional theatre. The geometry was an abstract summary of how we saw our material environment. In combining the rigidity of geometry with images of intense primitivism, Artaud hoped that the audience would lose its complacency towards the physical universe.

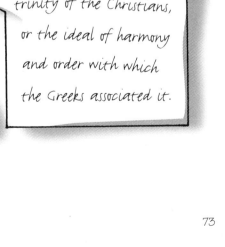

The number three used in groupings, has had religious connotations since antiquity. It is the holy trinity of the Christians, or the ideal of harmony and order with which the Greeks associated it.

The Cenci was performed seventeen times and then it closed. For Artaud this was the last straw after a string of disasters. He was physically weak. Theatre directors had no confidence in him. He had no money and staff and suppliers continually demanded payment. During this period, Artaud's face began to reflect the effect of so many difficulties. He developed a nervous twitch and seemed absent, detached from the world.

CHAPTER 4
Travelling

Mexico: Artaud's cruelty runs in the blood of the Indians

Staging *The Cenci* left Artaud in a state of social and material collapse. He now felt that his ideas on cruelty could be developed no further in Paris. So he began to think about other places. He had, since 1933, been making notes on ancient cultures from Greek books including *The Tibetan Book of the Dead*, the *Bhagavad Gita* and the Jewish cabbala. He left no stone unturned. He was interested in the rituals of Mexico's ancient cultures before Cortés' Conquest. He thought he would be able to find in them the primary forces that he sought. Perhaps they still flowed in the blood of the Mexican Indians, the only people that remained untainted by Western education.

In Mexico, the theatre that Artaud had in mind expressed itself directly, without the intervention of actors who could corrupt it.

Artaud believed that the culture of the colonisers was a negative force, whereas the conquered peoples reflected a profound knowledge. In Mexico, the proximity of the land, the flow of volcanic lava and the indigenous presence could help to cure the rift between body and soul, a wound that had been opened by the Europeans. Perhaps the Mexicans had a better understanding of how Artaud's theatre could bring energy back into a dead culture. In August 1935 he began to prepare a series of lectures that he was thinking of giving in Mexico.

Money problems once again

Artaud needed support for his journey: money and contacts in order to be able to give his lectures in Mexico where he planned to stay for some time. He visited several official departments, wanting his travels to be granted the status of a mission. This mission consisted of rescuing pre-Columbian cultures from the authorities. Finally, the Mexican Ambassador to France agreed to help. This assistance covered the cost of the journey but he set off with scarcely any money in January 1936.

I'm leaving to search for the impossible: the essence of the real human heart. A heart free of the chains of European words and thoughts.

A black sorcerer and the sword of Toledo

The ship on which Artaud was travelling was held up for nearly three days in Havana, Cuba. There, Artaud came into contact with a black sorcerer who presented him with a small sword from Toledo. This sword became one of Artaud's principal amulets. He was convinced that he held in his hands an object invested with extraordinary powers.

This sword represents for Artaud the first sign of the proximity of a different world.

Artaud landed in Mexico on 7 February 1936. He felt that he had been chosen to return the power of ancient magic to civilisations in decline. The night before he arrived, Artaud felt nervous and had a series of nightmares. He sensed that, somehow, his arrival in Mexico would herald a decisive experience in his life. Only twenty days after his arrival at the port of Veracruz, the Mexican press announced:

The Mexican public is invited to a series of lectures by Antonin Artaud. The distinguished French intellectual proposes to develop a series of talks on the following stimulating topics:

Surrealism and revolution
Man against destiny
Theatre and the gods

The talks will take place in the Department of Social Action at the University of Mexico City on 26, 27 and 29 March in the Bolívar Amphitheatre...

Se cree que la razón de que el escritor y tan Recalde encuentra...

> The mythology of Mexico's Indians holds the ancient secret of the race. Before the race disappears that ancient secret must be captured.

Artaud gave lectures to finance his stay. But he also hoped to convert people. He tried to teach the Mexican youth something. He wanted to introduce them to Surrealist ideas, bringing back the values of the displaced indigenous cultures. In his lecture 'Surrealism and Revolution' he did not attack the Marxist revolution in its entirety. He simply indicated that Communism dealt with humanity in a very partial way, ignoring man's spiritual development. In 'Man against Destiny' Artaud argued against a distorted notion of fate which was expressed through terrifying myths. The true purpose of myths was not to horrify, but to show that man ought not to fear fate but face it, however secret and dark his destiny might be.

A bad time to arrive

Artaud arrived in Mexico to speak about the destruction of a rationalist and technological culture that harmed man. At the same time, the Mexican authorities were trying to integrate the Indians into civilisation and technology, to mechanise the countryside and end the tribal customs of the indigenous peoples. In his talks, Artaud time and again criticised the way in which the Mexican government was going about the revolution. All his lectures were provocative. In his dissertation on 'Theatre and the Gods', Artaud put forward a truly revolutionary idea opposing the teaching of modern teachers. He said that

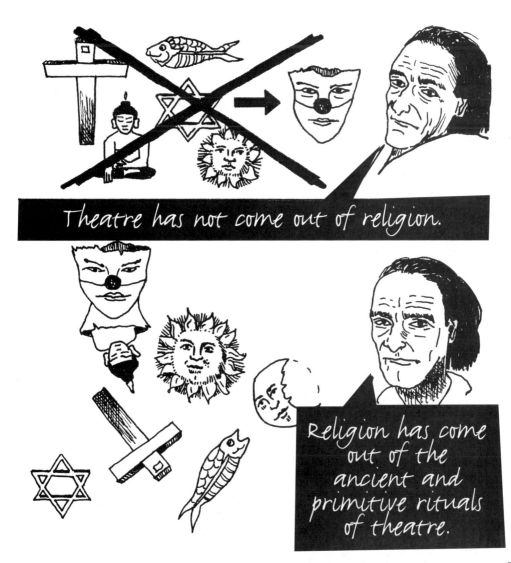

Theatre has not come out of religion.

Religion has come out of the ancient and primitive rituals of theatre.

Artaud gave a few more lectures. But he was essentially a man of action. He was tired of being in Mexico merely to hold forth about life in Paris or ideas on the new theatre from a university chair. He needed to find another way of dealing with the problem of the Indians. Two opportunities arose: one, at a conference on children's theatre, where he attended a puppet show; the other on a journey to Cuernavaca, a town near Mexico City.

My dear French friends,

After four months in Mexico, my situation is desperate.

I work for national newspapers in order to survive. But my real problem isn't financial. I came here to save the Mexicans, to stop them becoming more alienated from their ancient roots.

I urgently need to meet with certain indigenous tribes. I must learn their rituals and be initiated into their secret practices.

antonin artaud

Theatre has a potential for magic that no revolutionary government can ignore.

We must incorporate indigenous folk art into the art of the theatre. That's true revolution.

Artaud needed to contact the Indians directly to prove the effectiveness of his ideas about true revolution. An authentic uprising was not just to do with liberating the poor and oppressed classes. The Mexican Government had to stop considering the Indians an inferior race. Theatre needed to act as a means to transform society.

Artaud's articles in the Mexican press and his lectures brought him enough fame and prestige to enable him to ask for a grant to research the reality of life for the Tarahumara Indians. The grant was awarded and

Artaud travelled to Chihuahua, the nearest town to the area where the Indians lived. There he met a man of mixed Amerindian descent who accompanied him as guide for the rest of his journey.

Artaud wants to be initiated into the Tarahumara's rituals. He should be very careful. The Indians deeply distrust the white man.

To gain the Tarahumara's trust, you just have to show respect for the indigenous ways.

It's not just a question of trying peyote. It's to do with trying it in the place where peyote grows, where the act of taking it is sacred.

Accompanied by his guide, Artaud reached the Sierra Tarahumara. He very much wanted to take part in the peyote rite. The Indians called a plant with hallucinogenic properties 'peyote' or 'ciguri'. Artaud had heard about the rite. To him, peyote was not just a plant, it was about a principle of alchemy which could totally transform the mind.

Artaud was powerfully impressed by the spectacular scenery of the Sierra Tarahumara. It came as a revelation. He looked at rocks projecting two shadows on the ground shaped like animals. He seemed to see an animal devouring itself. Perhaps those shapes were natural, but it was the repetition of the pattern that was not natural. These same shapes were repeated by the Tarahumara in their rituals and dances and had not come into existence by chance; they obeyed the same secret mathematical rule, with the same aim of representing everything with its double.

Many trees in the Sierra Tarahumara are shaped like human beings. We're always face to face with someone identical.

Our dance formations aim to show the duality of things.

The Tarahumara guarded the 'double' carefully. To lose it meant to risk being disconnected from the world. Souls separated from their doubles were condemned to wander in the great void and finally they would be lost. Being lost meant having no relationship with the sacred forms of the universe. And every sacred form had its double.

Evil is no more than losing consciousness or becoming separated from the double.

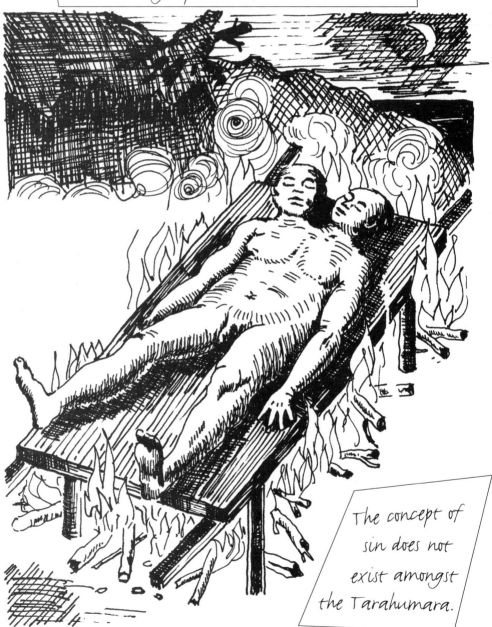

The concept of sin does not exist amongst the Tarahumara.

An apparently deceptive ceremony

The Indians welcomed Artaud warmly because it was he who got permission for them to perform the peyote rite. One of the government officials responsible for keeping order amongst the Tarahumara wanted to ban the rite but Artaud dissuaded him, saying that such a ban would certainly result in an Indian uprising. In gratitude, the Tarahumara allowed Artaud to participate in the ceremony. The Indian chief approached Artaud to open up his consciousness. The Tarahumara did this by cutting the skin with a knife between the heart and the arm.

I'll hardly touch you with the knife. It doesn't do any harm. Hardly a drop of blood will be shed.

I feel no pain. I feel as if I am waking up to something new. It's as if I'm being enveloped in a light that I've never seen before.

The setting of the ritual shows the new sun passing through seven points before lighting up the earth. Each cross symbolises one of those passages.

At sunrise, a man on horseback enters the circle of dancers. The horse represents the new sun on the surface of the earth.

After several days, Artaud met priests of the *Tutuguri*. The *Tutuguri* was one of the most esoteric rituals of the Tarahumara. *Tutuguri* meant 'the song of the owl' in the aboriginal language. Women also took part. The ritual was only ever performed at dawn and consisted of a dance to petition the sun. In 1948, Artaud wrote a poem about this experience called 'Tutuguri, the Rite of the Black Sun'.

Two days after the *Tutuguri* rite, Artaud used peyote and took part in the dance. In the centre of a circle marked out on the ground, there was a fire. Ten crosses were nailed down on the side where the sun rose. From each one a mirror was hung. The idea was that the whole ceremony would be reflected in these mirrors, so that it would also have its double.

The Tarahumara give a sacred meaning to different geometric figures. The form of man is also linked to this idea of a geometric universe.

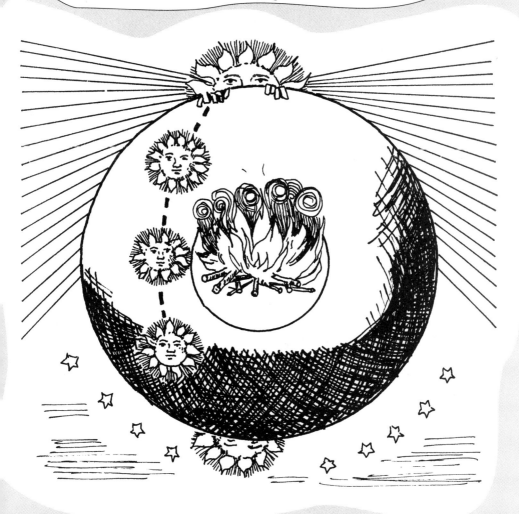

When the sun sets the sorcerer enters the circle.

The movements of the dance are frenetic. The Indians dance to rid themselves of visions and dark torments.

The sorcerers entered and left the circle. On the ground, at the foot of each sorcerer was a hole in which he placed a vessel. Over this vessel the sorcerer grated the peyote. The Indians used a kind of small stick as a rasp. It was this rasp, used in the correct way, that produced the curative effect of the peyote. The right to use the rasp was a privilege held only by the sorcerers. The dance continued until all the peyote had been distributed. Artaud described the peyote as a kind of sweet paste that produced a feeling of nausea. Each participant spat into the hole in the ground. This symbolised a purging that was only possible because of the magical effects of the peyote.

After taking the peyote, Artaud and many of the Indians fell into a deep sleep. The sorcerers woke them for the final cure. During this phase the priests shook the rasps over the heads of the initiates. Finally, came the water ceremony.

The Indians sprinkled water over the initates while uttering certain phrases to which they attributed magic powers. This was the final cure.

The visions stimulated by peyote are free of contradictions. After this experience, one can never again confuse lies with the truth.

After his stay with the Tarahumara, Artaud returned to Mexico City. Moved by what he had just experienced, he wrote several articles about indigenous rituals. This subject was repeated in many of his writings over the next years. The pieces were published separately, but in 1955 they were brought together in one book entitled *The Tarahumara*.

Artaud returned to Mexico City and very soon left for France. Once there, he renewed his love affair with Cécile Schramme. Artaud had known Cécile before setting off for Mexico. Now he decided to marry her and they got engaged. Once again, Artaud's addiction to opium disrupted his romantic plans. This time it was Cécile who convinced him to undergo a new detoxification treatment. It seemed that the treatment was achieving results. Then, in May 1937, Artaud travelled to Brussels to give a lecture. There he abandoned his prepared text and spoke about the Tarahumara. Artaud's behaviour towards the audience became increasingly hostile. On his return from Brussels, he broke off his engagement to Cécile Schramme.

Revealing the Indians' secret is like I have killed myself. We all have to kill ourselves symbolically if we want to be transformed into different beings.

Artaud ends his talk with harsh words and in a very nervous condition.

A gift with strange powers

In April 1937, a friend gave Artaud a strange wooden cane with thirteen knots as a gift. He had an iron tip put on the cane and when the iron hit the ground, sparks flew. Artaud attributed magic powers to the cane.

The ninth knot on the cane bears the magic symbol of lightning.

The Celts, ancient inhabitants of Ireland, have a culture rich in imagery and ritual that Artaud would like to know at first hand.

The Celtic culture considers writing unnecessary. It promotes the image over the word.

Many images in Celtic art coincide with the sacred idea of cruelty defended by Artaud.

Artaud was convinced that the cane had once belonged to St Patrick, the patron saint of Ireland. Extraordinary powers were attributed to the saint's cane and Artaud started to think about travelling to Ireland. He imagined the country as a land of legend and magic.

While he was planning his trip to Ireland, Artaud managed to publish another book called *The New Revelations of Being*. The ideas in this book were the result of a combination of experiences: the old attempt at the Theatre of Cruelty and the new experiences Artaud had had with the Indians. He expounded on these new concepts in a letter to Breton with whom he had renewed his old friendship.

Yes, my dear Breton. The time has come, as announced by the apocalypse when Christ, to punish his Church, will raise up a Furious One who will overthrow ALL churches and send the rite of the inititates back under the ground.

> Ritual is fundamental to the theatre.

The days of the false life we live as men are numbered.

A journey towards other mysteries

Artaud was not a man to waste a great deal of time on preparations. He decided to travel to Ireland and left France in August 1937. His mission was to return St Patrick's cane to the Irish. He also wanted to tread the soil where ancient Celtic rituals were practised.

Many Celtic rituals reveal the idea of the double. For example, this position forms part of a meditation technique.

Two men facing each other pull each others' beards. In this way they enter into contact with eternity.

The purpose of the journey to Mexico was to awaken the ancient gods who sleep in museums.

The journey to Ireland is the double of my journey to Mexico.

In Ireland I want to restore the strength of the ancient Celtic gods.

It has only been possible to reconstruct Artaud's route and his experiences in Ireland from the letters that he sent to his friends.

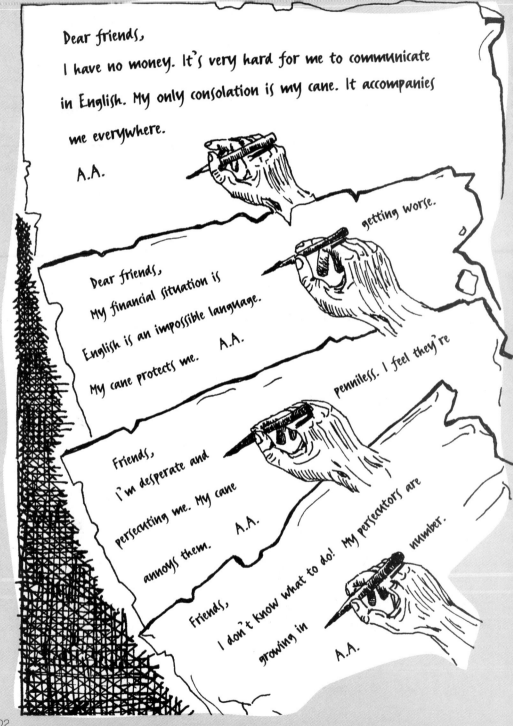

Dear friends,
I have no money. It's very hard for me to communicate in English. My only consolation is my cane. It accompanies me everywhere.
A.A.

Dear friends,
My financial situation is getting worse. English is an impossible language. My cane protects me. A.A.

Friends,
I'm desperate and penniless. I feel they're persecuting me. My cane annoys them. A.A.

Friends,
I don't know what to do! My persecutors are growing in number.
A.A.

I used my cane to impose silence on my persecutors.

In Dublin, Artaud caused a number of disturbances. He felt that he was being persecuted and had to defend himself. He walked through the streets brandishing his cane and was arrested on several occasions.

But Artaud was unable to protect his cane. On one occasion when he was arrested, the police confiscated it. The cane had attracted much attention from the Irish. It was not that it was really St Patrick's cane—that had been burned at the beginning of the sixteenth century. Still, the police reports called it 'the historic cane' and although they knew it was not true, the Irish *wanted* to believe in it.

Arrested and deported

After a succession of scandals, the police decided to imprison Artaud and deport him. Artaud was furious with the Irish, a people that could not understand the importance of his mission. He was determined not to return to Paris without having achieved his aim.

At the end of September 1937, Artaud was forced to return to France on board the *Washington*. He felt trapped. During the journey, a chief mechanic and a waiter approached his cabin. One of them held a wrench in his hand and Artaud thought that the two men were about to attack him. He tried to defend himself with the sword of Toledo given to him by the Cuban sorcerer and became very aggressive. They therefore decided that Artaud was dangerous and put him in a straitjacket.

CHAPTER 5

Asylums

Mental asylums would drive anyone mad

ON 29 SEPTEMBER 1937 ARTAUD was brought
ashore from the Washington. Not a single friend was
there to meet him. None of them was aware of the recent
events. He was taken to a psychiatric hospital near Rouen,
where he remained until April 1938, when he was transferred
to the Sainte-Anne hospital near Paris. There he was diagnosed as being incurably insane.

It seems this chap Artaud is going to spend a lot of time with us. He looks crazy to me.

The doctors are as ignorant as ever. They've diagnosed me as incurably insane.

At the beginning of 1939, Artaud was transferred again. Now he found himself in the Ville-Evrard asylum where he remained locked up for nearly four years. The situation in that asylum was disastrous. The physical ill-treatment and the deficiencies in medical attention made Artaud's mental condition worse. He was treated with utter cruelty. Very different from the liberating 'cruelty' which he had proposed for the theatre. When the doctors came up against a case they did not understand, their ignorance infuriated them and they became cruel. That is exactly what happened in Artaud's case.

Wartime

While Artaud was shut up in Ville-Evrard, World War II broke out. The world entered one of its most horrendous periods, with restrictions on food, rationing and a flourishing black market

Psychiatric patients are condemned to death by the Nazis.

We're hungry and frightened. Every day more and more inmates are dying from lack of food.

The power of spells

Imprisoned in the asylum, Artaud sent strange letters to his friends. He covered pieces of paper with magic symbols and then burned holes in them. He attributed the power of witchcraft or spells to his writing. The purpose of these spells was to protect and help those he loved.

Letter sent to Roger Blin, 1939
(from the original)

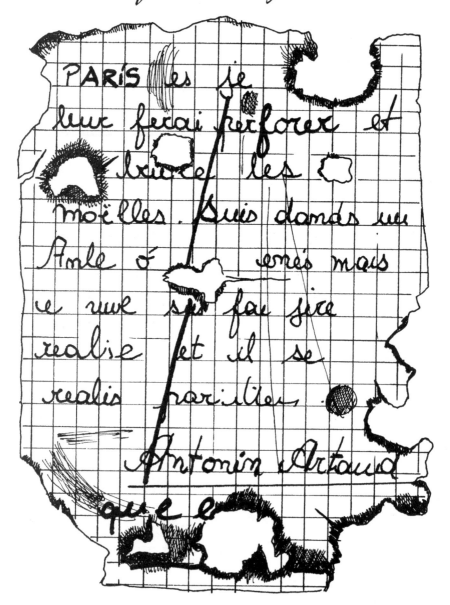

Letter sent to Jaqueline Breton, 1937 (from the original)

Letter sent to Sonia Mosse, 1939 (from the original)

Artaud had started sending these spells from Ireland and continued to do so during his confinements in psychiatric hospitals. In the asylum, the words, images and even his handwriting became more violent. The burning and the drawing were meant to show the inertia and impotence that Artaud felt. They also symbolised acts of aggression and purification.

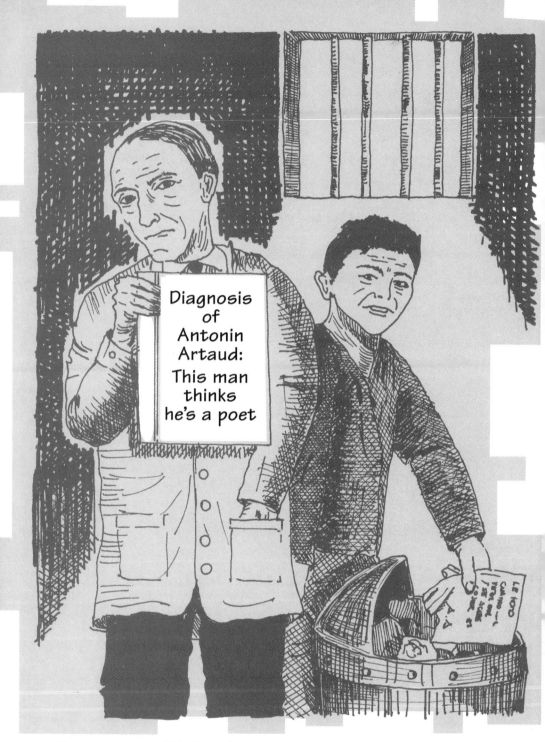

During his stay in Ville-Evrard, Artaud tried to continue writing. Apart from the letters sent to his friends, the rest of his writing has disappeared because the hospital staff systematically threw everything that Artaud wrote into the rubbish bin.

When his friend Robert Desnos found out about Artaud's situation, he sent a letter to Dr Gaston Ferdière who was an old ally of the Surrealists and was now director of a mental hospital. Desnos' letter was a plea for help. He, Paul Eluard and Jean Paulhan wanted to get Artaud transferred to a place where he would be better cared for.

Rodez: a more open prison

Eventually, Artaud's friends managed to have him transferred to the hospital at Rodez, under Ferdière. Rodez escaped the worst pressures of the war and Nazism, but it was still a mental hospital. Ferdière took responsibility for trying to heal Artaud.

I'm coming to Rodez a sick man. I wasn't sick when they shut me up in the first asylum. Mental hospitals have destroyed my mental health.

The first few times they used electroshock treatment, I gave my consent.

But after trying it once, I realise there's nothing more terrifying.

Dr Ferdière, poet and friend of the Surrealists, was also one of the exponents of the new electro-shock treatment. The technique involved applying electrical currents to different parts of the patient's brain. How this therapy worked was unknown. Nevertheless, during the nineteen months of his stay at Rodez, Artaud underwent more than fifty sessions. In one session, one of his vertebrae was fractured. Eventually, he lost all his teeth. But that did not deter Ferdière. He was prepared to try everything to cure Artaud.

Dr Ferdière did not rely on electro-shock therapy alone. He also persuaded Artaud to return to his writing, reading and drawing. Artaud translated Lewis Carroll as well as poems by Keats and Poe He also wrote many letters. Ferdière decided to grant Artaud some privileges. He let him have a room to himself and often invited him to dine with him. Even so, the relationship between doctor and patient was not easy. Ferdière considered Artaud a sick man. Artaud considered himself merely misunderstood.

LEWIS CARROLL

At Rodez, Artaud did the French adaptation of my book *Alice through the Looking-glass.*

He has adapted some of my writing. He is drawn to the drama and the violence.

He has also translated several of my poems.

KEATS

POE

Letters—an old habit

At Rodez, Artaud returned to his correspondence with friends, as well as the spells. He signed the letters written during his first months in the asylum 'Antonin Nalpas'. Nalpas was his mother's maiden name. Antonin explained the change of name by saying that Artaud had died in the mental hospital of Ville-Evrard in 1939 and Antonin Nalpas had been reincarnated in his body. In September 1937 he went back to signing his letters 'Artaud'. For Doctor Ferdière this was a sign of his recovery.

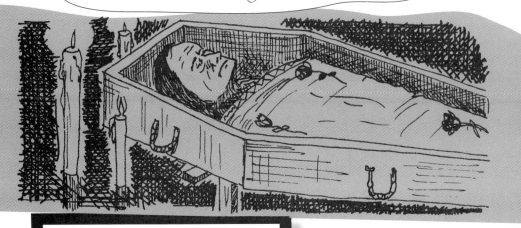

Antonin Artaud was assassinated by ill-treatment in the asylum of Ville-Evrard.

For now, I'm Antonin Nalpas. But I agree with all of that Artaud's ideas.

Self-portrait
(from the original)

The Immaculate Conception
(from the original)

The letters from Rodez were sent to his friends, family and to Dr Ferdière. One of the dominant themes in this correspondence was religion. Artaud referred a great deal to Jesus Christ and the religion of his childhood, which he seemed to have taken up again. Nevertheless, Artaud's religion was not that of an ordinary Catholic. At the same time as taking communion in the cathedral at Rodez, he continued to abuse the priests. He still believed that the world was dominated by occult forces. For Artaud, Jesus was among the great visionaries in the history of humanity.

Another very common topic in Artaud's letters was sexuality and the body. He completely rejected carnal love and everything physical. One must not forget that Artaud had suffered much physical pain. Electric shocks, hunger and incarceration had made him feel that his body was a curse. On leaving Rodez, his ideas about religion and sexuality changed radically.

First letter from Antonin Artaud to Dr Ferdière
(from the original)

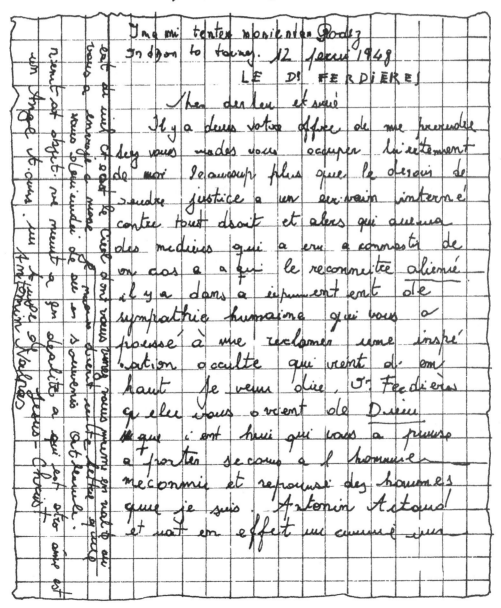

A language of his own

In Rodez Artaud kept a personal diary in which he recorded his experiences during his incarceration. After his death, the writings were published under the title *Notebooks from Rodez*. Both in his notebooks and in his letters, some words appear written in a language that is incomprehensible. The psychiatrists call this phenomenon *glossolalia*. Artaud and other patients invented a language that was meaningful for them alone. However, Artaud was not a simple psychotic. All his life he had sought to create a new language and he did not stop searching when he was locked up. He was trying to create a more effective form of expression than the language of known words.

Loje deber
loged tarbi

Lauish
bosh o i
georgir

A u o girgi
mazank aer

Self-portrait (from the original)

The faces of pain

Artaud had sketched since he was young. His drawings continued with spells illustrated with shapes and symbols that he had developed in Ireland.

When he was first incarcerated, he stopped sketching, but he went back to it at Rodez where he worked predominantly on portraits and sketches.

These drawings follow the same criteria as the 'cruelty' of the theatre.

The fractured and obsessive images recall the workings of dreams.

Illusions of the Soul (from the original)

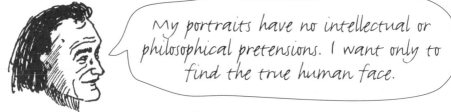

My portraits have no intellectual or philosophical pretensions. I want only to find the true human face.

For Artaud the human face is the space where the struggle between the forces of death can be observed.

The Blue Head (from the original)

Artaud did not seek to represent or describe anything in his sketches and portraits, any more than he did in acting and writing. His works were a magical gesture. Artaud lived this magic inside his body and afterwards emptied it out onto paper. The magic was an act which tried to restore a truth which would allow men to live in greater freedom.

The Projection of the True Body
(from the original)

Artaud and Europe liberated

The end of World War II in 1945 enabled Artaud's friends to visit him at Rodez. Among them were Roger Blin, Jean Dubuffet and Arthur Adamov. They managed to get permission for Artaud to leave the hospital from time to time, but he had to return to Rodez at night. Until he obtained this permission his friends had represented the only contact Artaud had with the outside world. Not all the news his friends brought was good. Some of his companions had died.

PAULE THÉVENIH

This is where Artaud lives until his death. In this clinic he returns to his intellectual work with zeal.

Ivry-sur-Seine clinic

In May 1946, Dr Ferdière felt that Artaud's mental state had improved. He decided to release him, but he stipulated as a condition that Artaud's friends should take responsibility for his financial needs. Paule Thévenin, a medical student, was given the task of getting a room for Artaud in a private clinic at Ivry-sur-Seine.

After Rodez, my face and my world have changed, and so...

...my outlook on the outside world can no longer be the same either.

Artaud's room at Ivry-sur-Seine

A group of friends organised fund-raising activities for Artaud. They arranged an auction of manuscripts and sketches donated by many artists and writers. Breton put on a play based on some of Artaud's writings. They also received donations from figures such as Picasso, Sartre and Simone de Beauvoir. In the clinic at Ivry, Artaud continued to draw portraits. He also started to write again. His writing after Rodez revealed profound changes compared to the period before his confinement.

CHAPTER 6
Religion

The rejection of myth

ARTAUD'S RESTORED MENTAL WELL-BEING was accompanied by a complete change of values. This transformation caused him to question many of the ideas of his youth. He rejected any myth or intellectual conception of the world. He recognised only facts and the reality of personal truths. He abandoned his leaning towards esoteric writings, oriental religions, the cabbala and myths.

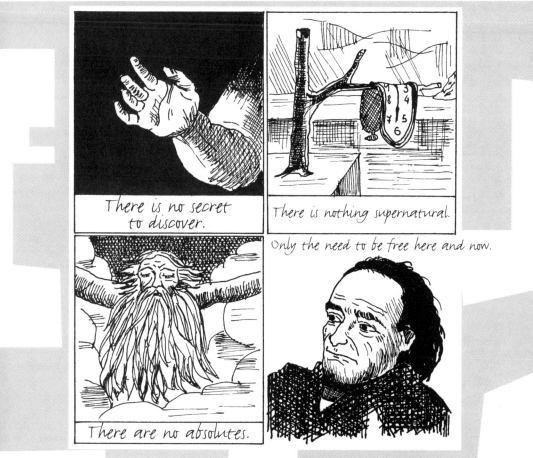

There is no secret to discover.

There is nothing supernatural.

Only the need to be free here and now.

There are no absolutes.

From the end of 1945, Artaud wanted to rid his writings of any trace of religion. He deliberately wrote 'god' in lower case. He amended his text 'The Peyote Rite' to eliminate any sign of Christian faith. He did not lose his belief in the divine, but he felt that the divine had been ruined by the 'god' of men.

Man's age-old interference has corrupted everything divine.

Artaud wants to get rid of the predominant idea of the 'man-god'.

The Peyote Rite

Artaud's aim was to restore the unity of good and evil, of the satanic and the divine. Man needed to have free access to the divine. Religion forced the faithful to fear God. The pacts of fear between gods and men destroyed all possibility of the divine.

There was another important characteristic in Artaud's writings after Rodez: the reassessment of the body in relation to the soul. Artaud considered that both the soul and conscience were phantasms that ruled the body and caused it suffering.

Artaud, the Momo

Between 1946 and 1948 Artaud produced many of his most important pieces. In September 1946 he wrote Artaud, the Mômo. By then, he had come a long way. He had experienced writing, theatre, drugs, lengthy travels and madness—all to try to make his idea of a new man concrete. It was this journey that was reflected in the poems in this new book.

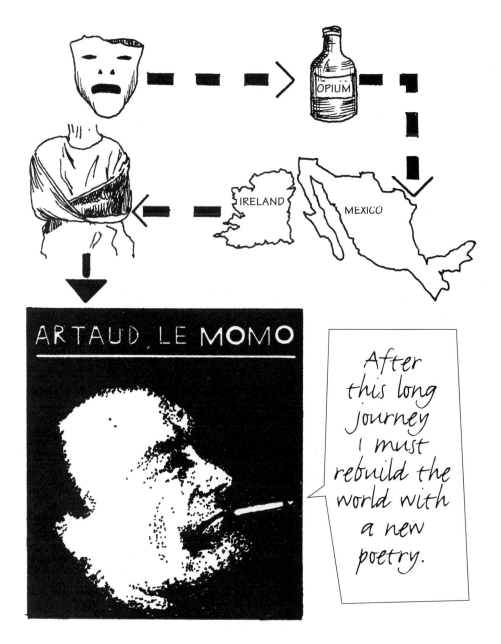

ARTAUD, LE MOMO

OPIUM

IRELAND

MEXICO

After this long journey I must rebuild the world with a new poetry.

In this book, Artaud proposed the remaking of the body. When Artaud referred to the body, he meant the world. He wanted to remake the world.

Normality, goodness and health are disguises which hide human misery.

Ranked against these disguises are illness, madness and Artaud's poetry.

Artaud knew that his evil was shared. His pain had a social origin. Anguish was a form of bodily suffering and not an act of the soul. The pain suffered by Artaud since childhood was produced by a society that had to castrate men and make them mad in order to survive, a society that was a madness machine.

In *Artaud, the Mômo* there was criticism of society's concept of the soul. It was believed that the soul was father of the body, that it was superior. For Artaud, that superiority was a lie. It was the deception that the authorities used to enslave men. This deception could be symbolised in various ways:

As if the body were the carriage and the spirit the mind...

...led by another spirit called the coachman.

Artaud turned society's accepted ideas upside-down. He said that 'the soul is born of the body, and not the body of the soul'. Work and a tired body maintained and fed the soul. Without the body the soul could not conceive of ideas or values, nor register information from reality. Without the body the soul could not even exist.

As if the 'body' were the body of all the soldiers killed under the orders of the great spirit, the general who makes them kill.

SPIRIT

Society imprisons or drives mad anyone it doesn't understand.

A sick society is one that doesn't accept the differences between people.

Madness is a kind of rebellion against the establishment.

In the poems in *Artaud, the Mômo*, Artaud expressed his views on his experiences in mental hospitals. He believed that asylums were alienated places where doctors practised black magic. Black magic was a means for psychiatrists to transform life into death. Medicine was a trap. It pretended to strive for man's good health, but its true intention was to eventually destroy those who had been beaten down or were different.

135

Artaud's new poetry was different from any poetry that had been written before. Its language was violent. It was filled with insults and terms that many called obscene or unpoetic. But Artaud's intention was to show that poetry did not depend on the use of pretty or dulcet words. For him, poetry implied risk. It was a way of giving form to man's despair or happiness. That form had to be intense. It was not meant to please readers but to stimulate them.

To stimulate is to show man as he is, with all his misery, his hatred and his greatness.

Intense writing never denies itself the chance to speak the truth.

Vieux-Colombier lecture

On 13 January 1947, Artaud announced a performance, 'The Story Lived by Artaud Mômo' at the Vieux Colombier theatre. It was his first public appearance after the nine years locked up in psychiatric hospitals. The hall was full, packed with his friends and those who were merely curious. There were also famous figures such as Picasso and the writers Sartre and Camus.

Many of us have come to listen to a great poet.

But there are those who've come to make fun of a madman. They'll be in for a surprise.

Artaud seems like a man from an unknown world who has come to make us see the true face of misery.

ANDRÉ GIDE

The performance at Vieux-Colombier lasted four hours. Those who had come to mock soon lost any desire to do so. Shortly after he had started reading, Artaud's words became punctuated with screams, writhing and wild gesticulation. Artaud performed as a true artist of the Theatre of Cruelty. The writer André Gide attended the performance and wrote a piece in which he described how moved he had been by seeing Artaud's desperate and ravaged face.

I'll never forgive this idiotic and thoughtless society for the nine years locked up in asylums.
Such an inefficient society that can't give anyone a good reason for living.
Leave me alone! My body and I don't want to be at the mercy of anyone.

At the end of this memorable event, the audience remained silent. They had been in the presence of a man who had been brutally beaten but was not yet burnt out. From his pain and suffering, Artaud had extracted a vital force that paralysed his audience.

Faced with a man who takes so many risks, I'm ashamed of the mediocrity of my own banal values.

Artaud's words shake us like an earthquake.

Van Gogh, the Man Suicided by Society

For André Breton *Van Gogh, the Man Suicided by Society* was Artaud's indisputable masterpiece. Certainly, the book is key to understanding Artaud's oeuvre. With *Van Gogh*, the Dutch painter, Artaud saw his own self reflected in a mirror. It's difficult to find a similar case of one man identifying so strongly with another.

As I research Van Gogh's work I feel as if I'm discovering myself.

Our destinies, our aims and our frustrations are so similar.

Artaud in poetry and theatre, Van Gogh in painting; they were two artists of genius, but genius always has its price. It is too different and dangerous for society. Both were misunderstood by the communities they had to live in. Both suffered illness and madness. Both had the same objective: to reach a higher level in art and in life.

Artaud defended madmen in this book. He wanted to justify the insanity of many who were marginalised. For Artaud a madman was a misunderstood genius. Society looked down on him and prevented him finding a place where he could develop his talents. The only escape for the genius was madness.

For society, curing a madman means making him fit into the very world that he rejects.

The only possible cure for a madman is for others to understand his need to be different.

For Artaud it was not the man they called mad who was abnormal, but the world around him.

Artaud came to Van Gogh's defence as a way of defending himself. What he wrote about the painter could also be applied to himself. Van Gogh was not crazy. His works attacked traditions, institutions and nature itself. After seeing one of Van Gogh's landscapes, nobody could view nature as they had before. Artaud was not crazy either. After reading one of his poems, nobody could think about poetry in the same way again.

Van Gogh's painting affects sight, hearing, smell and touch. It transforms the way we see the world.

Artaud called this book, *Van Gogh, the Man Suicided by Society* although, in fact, Van Gogh committed suicide. Artaud's view was that Van Gogh did not reach the decision to kill himself alone. He killed himself because society left him no choice.

Society was really his murderer. The 'suicide' was a punishment for having wanted to stand apart from accepted norms. Artaud described this criminal act against Van Gogh as an act of possession.

Artaud admired Van Gogh's style of painting whereby he used his 'own language'. This was achieved by using the basic elements of painting. To create a work of genius, Van Gogh needed only a paintbrush, a canvas, paint and the strength to pour his passion into the object he was painting. He did not use resources from other arts as tools. Neither history, nor personalities, nor world events were the most important elements on canvas. The image was the main protagonist. That 'own language' was the same that Artaud had claimed for the Theatre of Cruelty.

In Van Gogh's painting, grasp the image not the story.

In Artaud's theatre, grasp the gesture not the word.

For Artaud, after his stay in the asylums, there was no information of greater value than information about concrete reality. No myth, fable or god was more important than the objects closest to hand in life. Artaud felt that Van Gogh's painting showed that he shared this belief.

Van Gogh is able to transform daily objects into symbols of the whole universe.

HOLY BIBLE

Vincent

Artaud used *Van Gogh, the Man Suicided by Society* to once again pour out his hatred of psychiatry. He knew at first hand the incompetence of psychiatrists after his nine years of confinement. Van Gogh also suffered from the lack of understanding of various doctors and wrote about this in a letter to his brother Theo:

Dear Theo,

I don't think I can rely on my doctor at all. He seems to be sicker than me.

Vincent

Psychiatrists see every artist as an emeny.

Escaping from hell meant not deceiving oneself.
This was the struggle of every true artist and
Artaud and Van Gogh were true artists.

A new family

In the years following Rodez, Artaud rejected his family and attached himself to his friends. It was they who looked after his financial and emotional well-being. He never forgave his relatives for abandoning him while he was confined. He no longer even recognise any blood ties with them. When he referred to his sister Malausséna, he did so only to express his rejection.

I know I can depend on you. Whereas that Malausséna who says she's my sister is just an imposter.

Born again

In his poem 'Here lies', Artaud returned to a familiar theme from his early writings: the negation of the Father figure. But in this work he also negated the maternal image. Artaud completely rejected any idea of filial relationship.

I, Antonin Artaud am my own son, my father and my mother.

In the Theatre of Cruelty we must liberate ourselves from the power of the text.

In life we must struggle to not submit to the absolute power of the father's word.

To Artaud, his stays in mental asylums were a real experience of death. He continually repeated that he thought that his family's absence during this period made it an accomplice in his murder. He therefore needed to be reborn. Now it was Artaud who decided to cut himself off and to give his relatives up for dead. The idea of the symbolic assassination of the Father had already been described in the *Manifestos of Cruelty*. In Artaud's theatre it was the figure of the Author/Father that had to be abandoned.

To have done with the judgement of god

To have done with the judgement of god was the title of a poem that Artaud recorded for a French radio station on 15 September 1947. Several of his friends took part in the reading. There was no rehearsal, just a simple run-through before the recording.

The shouts and noises that accompanied the reading were improvised in the recording studio under Artaud's direction. He had set breathing exercises, teaching the actors to scream until they ran out of breath.

> Artaud makes us find the best way to shout or to read.

> To find the way means to understand. To understand is to be cured. From this comes the 'cruel cure' proposed by Artaud.

The first part of *To have done with the judgement of god* was a call to fight for man's liberation and a critique of imperialism and consumerism. The idea that the consumption of products was the path to happiness was destroying man. But much more destructive was the acceptance of an identity that culture imposed. That identity was the 'I', a product of an education that taught one to serve alien interests instead of choosing liberty.

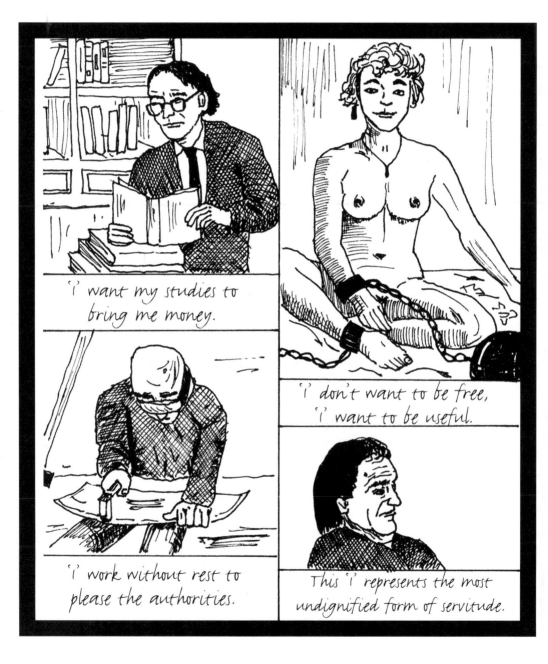

'I' want my studies to bring me money.

'I' don't want to be free, 'I' want to be useful.

'I' work without rest to please the authorities.

This 'I' represents the most undignified form of servitude.

Artaud's accusation was clear: society did not educate
men but soldiers, people who only knew how to defend
their secure place in the world with force and violence.
All idea of solidarity had been abandoned.

Artaud took his critique of theatre to the extreme in this work. He wanted to use the time left to him to divorce his 'cruelty' from other theories of how theatre should be. The years of confinement had not changed the beliefs he had held in his youth. In *To have done with the judgement of god*, Artaud declared himself an enemy of the theatre. He loved theatre and that was why he attacked it. And there was no contradiction: what he loved could only work if it underwent a complete transformation.

The history of the theatrical genre must end now.

I want a new theatre for a new man.

The vices of bad theatre must be radically eliminated.

Artaud is not a theorist of theatre.
He's a theorist of the destruction of theatre.

Everything inside me is as dark as the deepest night. But I'm going to transform the points of light of my internal night into poetry and rhythm.

There were fragments in this poem where Artaud returned to the topic of physical suffering. They were particularly moving since it was one of his last poems. Artaud was ill and fore-saw the approach of death. His poet-ry reached a peak of intensity, it be-came urgent and precise. The poem showed a man suffering great physi-cal pain. But his mind remained as lucid as ever.

Final days, final letters

Some time after he left the mental hospital, Artaud began to complain about intermittent pains in his intestines. Paule Thévenin and his family tried to persuade him to consult a doctor. Artaud had no faith in medicine and refused. He blamed the dietary deficiencies during his nine-year confined in asylums for having ruined his digestive system.

Quiet! Don't tell the doctors about me.

The pains got worse and the intestinal haemorrhaging began. Artaud was taking enormous quantities of drugs to ease his pain, with little success. Finally, Paule convinced him to see a specialist. A series of x-rays was carried out. Artaud awaited the results with his friend Paule. In the waiting room he seemed unconcerned about what the doctor might say. He started to talk about his one obsession: his art.

The doctor reassured Artaud. He advised rest and prescribed a treatment, but he then asked to speak in private with Paule Thévenin and revealed the truth: Artaud had cancer.

The tumour was advanced and inoperable. The doctor authorised Artaud to have all the laudanum necessary to relieve his pain.

'There's an animal inside me'

Paule was not mistaken. Although nobody revealed to Artaud the true nature of his illness, he knew. For several months he had been taking huge quantities of chloral which plunged him into a state of near unconsciousness, but reduced the pain.

During his final weeks, Artaud often repeated that he would write no more. He thought he had said everything necessary. He no longer carried the usual notebook in his jacket pocket. However, he did not stick to his decision. It was impossible for him to resist the urge to write.

I, Antonin Artaud, leave my work in the hands of my great friend.

These are, almost certainly, the last words he'll write.

PAULE THÉVENIN

The day before his death, he lunched with the Thévenin family. He asked them to buy official paper, then he began to write. He wanted to leave everything in order. He drew up an authority for Paule to oversee the publication of his books. He behaved very ceremoniously, reading aloud as he wrote. This was his theatrical farewell.

Choosing death

On the morning of 4 March 1948, the secretary of the clinic at Ivry telephoned Paule Thévenin. He told her of Artaud's death. The clinic's gardener had gone into Artaud's bedroom to take him breakfast. He had found him sitting at the bottom of his bed. He was dead. A few days before, Antonin had indicated that he did not want to sleep lying down. This wish was granted. At the moment of death, Artaud was alone, without witnesses. That was also his wish. He died as he had wanted. Perhaps he chose his moment of death too.

CHAPTER 7
Artaud's Legacy

In parallel with the development of the Theatre of Cruelty, similar ideas were appearing in other parts of the world. They all tried to achieve what Artaud called 'total theatre': an integrated and effective spectacle.

In Berlin, Erwin Piscator defended ideas very similar to Artaud's about getting rid of scenery. In Russia, Ysevolod Meyerhold and Vladimir Mayakovsky arrived at theatrical concepts closely resembling those of 'cruelty'.

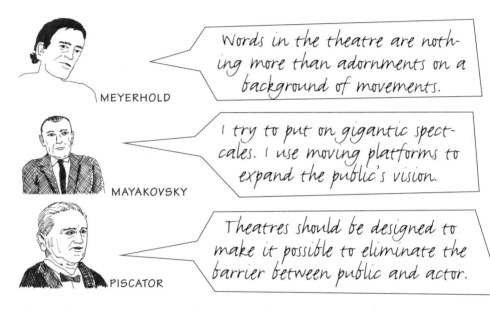

MEYERHOLD

Words in the theatre are nothing more than adornments on a background of movements.

MAYAKOVSKY

I try to put on gigantic spectcales. I use moving platforms to expand the public's vision.

PISCATOR

Theatres should be designed to make it possible to eliminate the barrier between public and actor.

In the 1950s the Theatre of the Absurd partly revived Artaud's ideas, trying to express the meaninglessness of existence and the anguish of the bourgeoisie faced with that meaninglessness. Samuel Beckett and Eugene Ionesco were two important exponents of this artistic movement. It was about a theatre that emphasised the need to destroy the fossilised language used by society. Like Artaud, the authors of the Absurd wanted to get rid of reverence for the text as the supreme element of the performance.

When we act, we speak using empty formulae, and automatic phrases. It's a parody of the way that society speaks. Our theatre promotes the non-literary elements of the production. It doesn't completely eliminate the text but it removes it from centre stage.

Scene from Beckett's Waiting for Godot.

Peter Brook: heir and critic

In the 1970s, Artaud's name cropped up constantly. In Great Britain the theories about cruelty were developed by one of the most important directors of the time: Peter Brook. He put on three Artaudian spectacles in London. One of them was Marat/Sade by Peter Weiss. Brook did not use Artaud's technique, which he regarded as out of date, but he revived the search for mystery that Artaud proposed for the theatre.

I agree with Artaud's aim of trying to reach all the spectator's senses.

PETER BROOK

Théâtre Panique

In the mid-1960s, the Spanish playwright Fernando Arrabal, the Chilean director Alejandro Jodorowsky and the French director Roland Topor created the *Théâtre Panique* which used humour, terror, sadism, confusion and blasphemy in order to shock. A man in *Panique* refused to consider art as separate from life. He lived as he acted, wrote or painted. This concept completely coincided with Artaud's own ideas.

To be 'Artaudian' means to risk everything in each performance.

The influence of the theatre and the figure of Artaud has endured until today. His name remains linked to the idea of the scream, to despair, to tortured poetry and to art as a form of liberation. Artaud's aim was not to teach any lesson about life. He chose not to accept any limitation imposed on him, but marked out the boundaries of his world. His work and life do not invite imitation—he despised imitation. Artaud's life and work offer one possibility. The possibility of total rebellion.

Eliminating the barriers between life and work involves great risk. I'm not trying to set an example. This is my choice. I've taken it to its final conclusion.

Index

Bibliography

Books by Antonin Artaud in English

Antonin Artaud: Anthology (ed. Jack Hirschman), City Lights Books, 1965
Antonin Artaud: Four Texts (tr. Clayton Eshleman & Norman Glass), Panjandrum Books, 1982
Artaud on Theatre (ed. Claude Schumacher), Methuen Drama, 1989
Artaud the Momo, Black Sparrow Press, 1976
Collected Works, Volums 1-5, John Calder, 1964-1974
The Peyote Dance (tr. Helen Weaver), Farrar, Straus & Giroux, 1976
Selected Writings (ed. Susan Sontag), Farrar, Straus & Giroux, 1976
The Theatre and its Double (tr. Victor Corti), Grove Press, 1958/Calder and Boyards, 1970
Watchfields & Rack Screams: Works from the final period, (ed. & tr. Clayton Eshleman & Bernard Bador), Exact Change, 1995

Books about Antonin Artaud

Barber, Stephen, *Antonin Artaud: Blows and Bombs*, Faber and Faber, 1993
Bermel, Albert, *Artaud's Theatre of Cruelty*, Taplinger Publishing Co, 1977
Derrida, Jacques & Thévenin, Paule, *The Secret Art of Antonin Artaud*, MIT Press, 1998
Costich, Julia Field, *Antonin Artaud*, Twayne, 1978
Esslin, Martin, *Artaud*, Fontana/Collins/John Calder, 1976
Goodall, Jane, *Artaud and the Gnostic Drama*, Clarendon Press/OUP, 1994
Greene, Naomi, *Antonin Artaud: Poet Without Words*, Simon & Schuster, 1971
Hayman, Ronald, *Artaud and After*, Oxford University Press, 1977
Knapp, Bettina, *Antonin Artaud: Man of Vision*, Swallow Press, 1980
Marowitz, Charles, *Artaud at Rodez*, M. Boyars/Drama Book Specialists, 1977
Plunka, Gene A., *Antonin Artaud and the Modern Theatre*, Fairleigh Dickinson University Press, 1994
Rowell, Margit ed., *Antonin Artaud: Works on Paper*, (exhibition catalogue), MOMA/Harry N. Abrams, 1966
Stout, John C., *Antonin Artaud's Alternate Genealogies: Self-Portraits and Family Romances*, Wilfred Laurier University Press, 1996

About the Authors

Gabriela Stoppelman has published three books of poetry and reviews Argentinian writers for the journal *Tamaño oficio*. She also contributes to the publication *Francachela*, which brings together writers from Chile, Argentina and Peru.

Jorge Hardmeier studied architecture at the University of Buenos Aires. He is the author of *Sobrespejos*, a collection of stories, and is a regular contributor to *Tamaño oficio*. He has illustrated several books on rock music and comics.